CHOICES
OF THE
CHOSEN

LESSONS FROM ISRAEL'S SHEPHERD KING

MARTY BERGLUND
GLENN KANTNER

PUBLICATIONS

Fort Washington, PA 19034

Choices of the Chosen

Published by CLC Publications

U.S.A.
P.O. Box 1449, Fort Washington, PA 19034

GREAT BRITAIN
51 The Dean, Alresford, Hants. SO24 9BJ

© 2012 by CLC Publications
All rights reserved. Published 2013

Printed in the United States of America

19 18 17 16 15 14 13 12 11   1 2 3 4 5 6

ISBN-10 (trade paper): 1-61958-056-X
ISBN-13 (trade paper): 978-1-61958-056-5
ISBN-13 (e-book): 978-1-61958-069-5

Italics in Scripture quotations are the emphasis of the author.

Contents

Praise for **Choices of the Chosen**

Sometimes the best lessons are learned from a good example. In Choices of the Chosen, Marty Berglund, Glenn Kanter and Nick Simpson have lifted examples from the life of King David of Israel—a man after God's heart—and organized them in bite-sized and believable portions. Following the course of a disciple from hearing the call of God through temptation and failure to enduring the most difficult challenges, David's life illustrates the real life of a believer. Every chapter includes a lesson and application—prayer to live out the timeless truth of Scripture. This book is a practical guide for all who wish to live a godly life in our turbulent world.

Dr. Gary Benedict
President, US Christian and Missionary Alliance (C&MA)

If you want to be challenged to increase your passion for God and improve on your service to Him, you will be inspired by anything spoken or written by Marty Berglund. I have always enjoyed my conversations with Marty because of his ability as a leader to bring out the best in me. What he says in this book will spur you on in your desire to pursue a love relationship with God!

Rev. Brent K. Haggerty
Lead Pastor, Stonecrest Community Church, Warren, NJ

Called "a man after God's own heart," King David is arguably one of the most well-known characters of the Bible. His success, amazing feats, faith in God, willingness to obey and even face his failures, seems beyond the possibility for us. Marty, however, brilliantly portrays David in a way that makes you feel like he is no different than you or me! The point being that we too can be men and women "after God's own heart."

Dr. David Smith
Lead Pastor, Fairhaven Church

Choices of the Chosen illuminates the life choices of David, "a man after God's own heart." In this study, we learn from David's good and bad decisions how imperfect people can make life choices that please God and bless us. Marty Berglund, Glenn Kantner, and Nick Simpson give us an honest, personal understanding of what it means to choose to live for God.in the real world of the 21st Century."

Chuck Tyree
Senior Pastor, Norwich Alliance Church, Norwich, CT

Marty has been a great friend to me over the years and an even better voice of reason. HIS realness, along with his gentleness and compassion, has taught me patience and humbleness in my own life. I can think of no one more gifted than Marty to write a book about King David; he too is a man who has lived his life seeking God's own heart in everything he does. From the initial response of the Lord's call on his own life, to persevering beyond the attacks from the enemy, Marty has always chosen to trust in the Lord and obey. He chooses to stay focused on the Lord Most High, rather than the obstacles he or the church faces.

Marty has always been a servant of Christ who looks at what's right in the eyes of the Lord rather than the eyes of the people. He never loses sight of the truth. He is a visionary who does not see success, but one who seeks only the will of Christ. Marty's words and thoughts can only help others draw nearer to our Lord and Savior Jesus Christ.

Mike Dryburgh
King of Kings Community Church, Manahawkin, NJ

The Case for *Choices of the Chosen*

David, the shepherd boy who became king of Israel, was a man esteemed by God. There were certainly other people in Scripture commended by the Lord, each with their own exemplary characteristics. However, David was known for being a man after God's own heart.

He wasn't perfect. In fact, as we visit portions of the Old Testament that tell his story, we'll learn quite a few lessons from the poor choices he made as well as from his successes. But his heart was turned toward the Lord and that caught God's attention. There is much to learn from David's path toward kingship and beyond so let's get started!

CHAPTER ONE

DAVID'S ANOINTING:
POSITIONING THE HEART FOR GOD'S CALL
1 Samuel 16:1–13

Pastor Marty Berglund

But the LORD said to Samuel, "Do not look on his appearance or on the height of his stature, because I have rejected him. For the LORD sees not as man sees: man looks on the outward appearance, but the LORD looks on the heart."
1 Samuel 16:7

God has placed a calling on each of our lives. Sometimes we may wonder whether or not we've heard His call, because we don't understand how He speaks. The term "call" in this context can often be confusing. We're not talking about a phone call or a bird call. We are talking about the leading of the Lord.

God reveals His plan for us by speaking to our hearts. That being said, it's important to position our hearts—to tune our ears, if you will—to recognize His voice. This means listening for Him to speak in sometimes unexpected ways. Beyond being unexpected, the call of God may not even be what we think we want. Yet if we listen and obey, God will bless the results.

David's Call

King David heard the call of God on his life, and he followed it. He is described twice in Scripture as a man after God's own heart. In First Samuel 16, God says that He picked David because of his heart. The heart's position seems to be a common theme and one we will examine as we look at David's life. Let's explore the different parts of David's heart that pleased and displeased the Lord so that we can better understand how to follow God's desires for our own lives.

We too can become people after God's own heart—knowing His plans and following His will. The first requisite for knowing God's will is having an open heart. Before David's reign Saul was the king of Israel. But Saul angered the Lord by blatantly disobeying God's instructions. (Saul saved the best livestock and plunder after defeating the Amalekites, when he had been told to destroy everything. You can read the story for yourself in First Samuel 15.) Because Saul violated God's will and closed his heart to the things of God, he lost his favor with God and his kingship rights.

God didn't audibly talk to David when he called him. He used someone else, a prophet, to speak His word into David's life. In First Samuel 16 God sent Samuel to Bethlehem to identify and anoint the next king—one with a heart to follow Him. When Samuel entered the town, he obeyed God's command to sacrifice a heifer and to call the family of Jesse before him. As soon as Samuel saw Jesse's oldest son, Eliab, the prophet decided Eliab had to be the right guy. In Samuel's time, as in most cultures throughout history, three things were highly esteemed: beauty, brains and brawn. In that respect the culture was similar to America's entertainment-saturated culture that's all about who's the prettiest, the coolest, the wealthiest, the most talented and so on. So when Samuel looked at Eliab, he thought, *Look at him! He's got it all. Surely he's the one the Lord will choose for the job.*

I can relate to Samuel. When I look at a young person, I often find myself thinking, *Wow, that kid's got potential. I hope he gets his life together and follows the Lord, because he could really do something great.* But look back at First Samuel: "But the LORD said to Samuel, 'Do not look on his appearance or on the height of his stature, because I have rejected him. For the LORD sees not as man sees. Man looks on the outward appearance, but the LORD looks on the heart'" (16:7). Samuel might have thought that Eliab was the total package—personable, good-looking, strong—but God was judging by a different scale and had someone else in mind.

Seven of Jesse's sons passed before Samuel, yet Samuel said, "The LORD has not chosen these" (16:10). Finally Samuel asked, "Are *all* your sons here?" Jesse mentioned that his youngest was out watching the sheep, and Samuel said, "Send and get him, for we will not sit down till he comes here" (16:11). So Jesse sent for David, and when David came in, the Lord said, "Arise, anoint him, for this is he" (16:12).

It's clear from this passage that Eliab and his brothers were not rejected because of their appearance but because of their hearts. And it's equally clear that David was anointed not because of his appearance (even though Samuel recognized that he was handsome) but because of his heart. This reminds me of Second Chronicles 16:9: "For the eyes of the LORD run to and fro throughout the whole earth, to give strong support to those whose heart is blameless toward him." Notice that the eyes of the Lord go to and fro, just looking for an open heart that He can move into—a heart like David's.

Later in this book we'll investigate the famous story of David and Goliath. The secret to David's victory over Goliath wasn't his strength. It wasn't his brains. It wasn't his beauty. It was his heart that was open to God. The secret to his success in everything he did—winning battle after battle and being followed and trusted by so many—was his heart. In fact, the reason the Bible makes such a big deal about David is because he had a heart for God. It was the secret to his success, and it's the secret to ours as well.

David was far from perfect. But God was not, nor is He

now, looking for angels in the flesh. He is searching for people He can use; for hearts that are open to His ways. The biggest question is this: are our hearts open or closed to God's call?

How Do We Open Our Hearts to God?

My friend Cedric played in the NFL for the Philadelphia Eagles in the 1980s. During this time, God said to him, "Cedric, now that you're a Christian, I'm choosing you. I'm anointing you to start a church in Lindenwold, New Jersey." That was a huge change and commitment for Cedric! But he listened to God and chose some great "players" to help him execute the vision God had given him, and now he's the pastor of a thriving church in New Jersey. I'm sure Cedric never expected to be playing on this kind of field. He went from being a defensive back to preaching behind the pulpit, yet one thing is clear: God had big plans for him!

I have another friend named Ed who worked as an engineer for many years. Ed accepted Christ in his forties and started attending church with his wife and their three boys soon after. Before long, God revealed to Ed that He'd chosen and anointed him to help me and others start a new church, the Fellowship Alliance Church in Medford, New Jersey. Ed had great organizational and managerial skills—gifts I don't possess. Our church, I believe, wouldn't be here today if it weren't for Ed.

I think people like Cedric and Ed clearly understand who they are. They heard God calling them, and they opened their heart to that call. That's why God is so greatly using them.

God doesn't just call big-name athletes or preachers. As He did with David, He can call a young shepherd roaming around the back side of a mountain. God calls everyone who is a Christian, and He equips all His people to live up to their special purposes in Him. When we follow Him, we find that being in the right place is far superior to being in what we *thought* was the best place.

I'm amazed by how many Christians don't seem to know who they are, what they're supposed to be doing or where they're going. Gary Benedict, the president of the Christian and Missionary Alliance, has called the American church a "sleeping giant." I agree. If churchgoers would recognize who God has called them to be and would open their hearts in a step of faith to say, "Okay, Lord, use me," it would be phenomenal. God would move in a mighty way.

So what does it mean exactly to open our hearts to God? The Bible uses the word "heart" to mean our inner, private world—the things that we think and feel every day that maybe even our best friend or our spouse doesn't know about.

The unfortunate thing is that we're predisposed to have closed-off hearts. As sinful beings, we're naturally concerned with *our* agenda and *our* happiness and how things work out for *us*. No one is naturally open-hearted toward God. Even my little grandkids, cute as they are, can be pretty selfish and deceitful. David wrote, "Behold, I was brought forth in iniquity, and in sin did my mother conceive me" (Ps. 51:5).

David understood his fallen human nature, but he also recognized that God could renew him from the inside out. For our hearts to be open, we first have to repent. We have to bend our knees and ask for and accept God's forgiveness. Jesus Christ and His sacrifice is our only hope—and the only key to eternal life. Being open and available for God to work starts with falling before Him and admitting that we have sinned and that He alone can save us.

Recognizing God's Call

When our heart is open to God, we're able to *hear* His call, but we also need to *recognize* His voice. To do so, we have to actively seek to discern how the Lord is speaking.

The process of recognizing and obeying God's leading is

threefold. First, we have to recognize that we have been *chosen* by God. Look at First Samuel 16:8–10: "Then Jesse called Abinadab and made him pass before Samuel. And he said, 'Neither has the LORD chosen this one.' Then Jesse then made Shammah pass by. And he said, 'Neither has the LORD chosen this one.' And Jesse made seven of his sons pass before Samuel. And Samuel said to Jesse, 'The LORD has not chosen these.'" Through the prophet Samuel, the Lord repeatedly uses the word "chosen" to indicate whom He had selected. The second a person prays to accept Christ, God claims that person as one of His own—He chooses him or her.

First Samuel 16 continues, "And the LORD said, 'Arise, anoint [David]; for this is he.' Then Samuel took the horn of oil and anointed him in the midst of his brothers. And the Spirit of the LORD rushed upon David from that day forward" (16:12–13). Once God has called, or chosen, us, we need secondly to be anointed. I'm not saying that we all have to be doused in oil poured from a horn, but we do need to realize that God has set us apart for a purpose. Samuel anointed David to help him recognize who he was—one chosen by the Lord.

The third step is an incredibly exciting one. Scripture tells us that the Holy Spirit—the very Spirit of God—came upon David. Wow! The Spirit quickly and fully filled David. He had the power of the Holy Spirit—teaching him, speaking to him, directing him—working in his life in powerful ways. When we as believers are filled with the Holy Spirit, we will recognize the leading of God in our lives and be able to obey His will.

Before Christ died and rose again, He told His disciples to obey the commands He had given them and to lead lives worthy of their calling. And He encouraged them by promising, "Truly, truly, I say to you, whoever believes in me will also do the works that I do; and greater works than these will he do, because I am going to the Father. . . . I will ask the Father, and he will give you another Helper, to be with you forever, even the Spirit of truth"

(John 14:12, 16–17). The Spirit enables us to remember Christ's teachings and to live out God's commands.

What happened to David happens to every person who comes to believe in Jesus Christ. When we receive Jesus, we are chosen by God, anointed for service and filled with the Holy Spirit. As believers, we can now recognize God's call on our lives and begin to follow His leading.

Opening Our Hearts and Living According to Our Calling

As important as it is to take that first step and to accept Jesus Christ as Lord and Savior, there's more for us to do as we seek to follow God's call on our lives. Accepting Christ is not a once-and-done event; the Lord wants to continually refresh and grow us. I've been a Christian for more than thirty years, and I've learned that opening my heart to God involves daily effort. The pressures of the world, the flesh and the devil all conspire to close our hearts to God's call, and we have to be dedicated to listening. Luke 11:28 tells us, "Blessed . . . are those who hear the word of God and keep it."

Keeping an open heart requires dedication and discipline. My wife and I both spend time in the Word. It's part of our daily life. We're targeting our hearts and aligning them with God's call.

I also pray every day. I have a time of meditation on God's Word *every day*. Why? In addition to loving spending time with my Father, I recognize that my heart is, as the hymn "Come Thou Fount" says, prone to wander. In order to keep my heart centered on God, I listen to other preachers' messages, and I talk about spiritual things and pray with my friends. All Christians need to practice these disciplines.

The Lord is reaching down, going through all the earth, asking, "Whose heart can I grab hold of? Who is open to being used?" Most hearts aren't readily given. Jesus clarified this when

He said that the pathway to heaven is narrow. The majority of people are going to take the broad path of selfish motives and closed hearts. But God will use the heart that's open to Him. When we feel helpless and don't know what to do next in our search for God's plan, He'll hold us in the palm of His hand and give us peace and a purpose. That's just who God is. Are we willing to let Him work?

Just like David, we're the chosen. We're the anointed. We're the ones the Holy Spirit works through to accomplish God's will in the world. Do we recognize our calling? God has selected each of us for a purpose and has given us individual spiritual gifts that He intends for us to use to further His kingdom. All it takes for us to discover God's call on our lives is a heart that's open toward Him. He'll show us His ordained plan for our service to Him.

Using our God-given gifts doesn't mean we all have to become pastors or go overseas to do missions work. My dad listened to the Lord, yet his life was far from glamorous. Instead of graduating from high school, Dad went off to fight in World War II and then came back and worked in a factory. Early on, Dad heard the Lord calling him to teach young boys, and he responded. For most of his life, he served as a Sunday school teacher for fourth-grade boys. When those kids grew up, they stayed in touch with my dad. Many of them brought their first cars by the house to show Mr. Berglund. My father had a huge impact on those boys, because he heard God's call on his life, recognized it for what it was and used the gifts God had given him, right where he was.

In Greek, the term *charisma* ("gift") has the same root as the word for "joy"—*chara*. In other words, we will experience joy when we use the gifts with which God has blessed us. We don't have to be preachers or doctors or engineers. He calls everyone who's a Christian. We just have to listen.

Let's pray:

God, show me where my heart is closed, and help me open it to You. I come before You with a repentant spirit. Forgive me for how I've turned my back on You, and help me discern Your voice. Are You speaking to me about my gifting, my talents, my abilities, my anointing? I surrender to the work of the Holy Spirit. Let me hear Your call; I will follow. Amen.

CHAPTER TWO

DAVID'S CONTEMPLATION OF THE LORD: RESPONDING TO GOD

Psalm 19

Pastor Nick Simpson

Let the words of my mouth and the meditation of my heart be acceptable in your sight, O LORD, my rock and my redeemer.
Psalm 19:14

In this book we're examining David, but not because he was an exemplary man who got everything just right. Not at all. David was a man who responded to the Lord in all sorts of ways, and many of those ways weren't positive. Yet God still called David a man after His own heart and anointed him for a specific purpose. It wasn't because David was special; it was because God had a plan for David. All David did was respond to God's calling in the right ways.

God has a plan for each of us too. God formed us in His image (see Gen. 1:26), and He longs to be in relationship with us. We were created to respond to God. Responding to God doesn't just mean talking to God, although it may involve that. It means that our entire lives should be in communion with God; everything we do should be in reaction to what He has done for us and who He has created us to be.

I believe God wants to show us, through David, that they

way for us to respond to life's trials is to respond first to God. God longs to help us navigate our finances, our marriages and our work routines.

David Responds to God's Being

We could spend a lifetime contemplating the majesty of God and His creation and never run out of new things to discover. God is glorified when we delight in Him and His works. David recognized the beauty and greatness of God, and his heart overflowed to God in an expression of worship and praise. It's important for us, like David, to respond to who God simply for who He is. Let's look at a psalm of David's:

> The heavens declare the glory of God,
> and the sky above proclaims his handiwork.
> Day to day pours out speech,
> and night to night reveals knowledge.
> There is no speech, nor are there words,
> whose voice is not heard.
> Their voice goes out through all the earth,
> and their words to the end of the world.
> In them he has set a tent for the sun,
> which comes out like a bridegroom leaving his chamber,
> and, like a strong man, runs its course with joy.
> Its rising is from the end of the heavens,
> and its circuit to the end of them,
> and there is nothing hidden from its heat. (19:1–6)

As David contemplated the vastness of who God is, he came to the realization that God is present everywhere—in the sky, in the day and the night, throughout the world— and He longs to make Himself known to everyone. David's response of worship to the greatness of God makes it clear that we are meant to respond, first and foremost, to God's being. In the last chapter we saw that David was anointed by God—and chosen to be king, no less—and what's so interesting is that David didn't immediately put a bejeweled crown on his head and sit on a kingly throne. It wasn't time for him to rule Israel yet, so he responded to God's anointing by contentedly going back to tending his sheep. David's heart was to worship God, to respond to God Himself, wherever God placed him.

It was out in the fields that David had confronted the greatness of the Lord and been moved to his response of worship. Nature is filled with the markings of God's beauty. Think about it. Very early mornings start out crisp and dark. Then, as the sun begins to rise, a red hue spreads across the heavens, and as the sun continues its ascent, the sky turns the bluest of blues. At night, after the sun sets, the heavens open up. Stars—a vast canopy of millions of pinprick lights—are everywhere; it's breathtaking. These are the things David saw every day as he stood watch over his sheep. He watched the morning's cool dew burn off in the sun's heat, and he heard chirping birds and symphonies of cicadas. In Psalm 19 we see that David realized that he was created to respond to his Creator, to the God he saw and felt and heard in everything that surrounded him.

Through His creation God makes Himself known to us, and it's our job to respond to that revelation. Paul asserts in Romans 1:20, "For his invisible attributes, namely, his eternal power and divine nature, have been clearly perceived, ever since the creation of the world, in the things that have been made" (ESV). It's comforting to me to know I serve a God who is everywhere; there is nowhere I can go to escape His vast being.

Paul and David knew that we are made to respond to God. But so often we respond not to God, who is the Creator of heaven and earth but to our own situations and circumstances. We start looking inward, and life becomes all about us. But God is telling us in Psalm 19, "I want you to respond to Me. I created you to commune with Me daily. Stop looking downward and inward; set your sights on My higher purposes!"

Sometimes we become overwhelmed by life's pressures. We get stuck focusing inward, looking to our own experience for answers. When we do this, we find out quickly that we can't handle things on our own. But when we set our focus on God—acknowledging His presence and providence in all things—He dwells within us and fills our hearts with peace.

David Responds to God's Word

God wants to be intimately involved in our lives. This is why He gave us, among other things, His Word. The Bible tells us about who God is and about His purpose for our lives. Besides seeing God in creation, David saw how God revealed Himself through His words. Look at the next section of Psalm 19:

> The law of the LORD is perfect,
> > reviving the soul.
> The testimony of the LORD is sure,
> > making wise the simple.
> The precepts of the LORD are right,
> > rejoicing the heart.
> The commandment of the LORD is pure,
> > enlightening the eyes.
> The fear of the LORD is clean,
> > enduring forever.
> The rules of the LORD are true
> > and righteous altogether.
> More to be desired are they than gold,
> > even much fine gold;
> sweeter also than honey,
> > and drippings of the honeycomb.
> Moreover, by them is your servant warned;
> > in keeping them there is great reward.
>
> Who can discern his errors?
> > Declare me innocent from hidden faults.
> Keep back your servant also from presumptuous sins;

let them not have dominion over me!
Then I shall be blameless,
　　and innocent of great transgression.

Let the words of my mouth and the meditation of my heart
　　be acceptable in your sight,
　　O Lord, my rock and my redeemer. (19:7–14)

For David God's Word was another way that God was revealing Himself and saying, "I want you to respond to Me." David recognized that the law of the Lord was perfect, right and clean, and he responded to God's Word by asserting his desire to follow it.

However, David's realization of God's greatness as expressed in His Word also made him very aware of his own sinfulness. David knew that his heart was naturally closed to the things of the Lord and that he needed to seek God's help to overcome his human tendency to stray. So David asked God to forgive him of his hidden faults and to keep him from willfully sinning.

David knew that sin is dangerous. It always damages us more than we realize, and every "small" sin opens the door for more serious ones. An addict doesn't wake up one morning and say, "I think I'll get addicted to something today." Instead, that person makes a series of decisions that slowly develop into an addiction.

Take a man addicted to pornography, for example. One day he may have been surfing the Internet and got bored or tempted and thought, *I'm going to take a look at this website, just this once. There's no one else home, so nobody ever has to know.* He seemed to get away with it, so he went back to look at the same website the following week, and he seemed to get away with it again. Eventually, once a week turned into three times a week. Three times a week turned into every day, which turned into a habitual pattern. Because the man responded to what the world told him was okay instead of responding to the principles in God's Word, he became trapped in sin.

Porn and other pleasures might provide an immediate release from the pressures of life—but they don't provide the pleasure or joy that God wants to give. Pleasure is temporary, which is why the addict has to keep going back to it over and over again. Eventually it fails to fill the emptiness, so the porn addict starts going to strip clubs or sleeping with prostitutes. The next thing he knows, he's looking back on his life, wondering, *How did I get here?* He got there by focusing on his own desires instead of meditating on the Lord's attributes as expressed in His Word and then seeking His will. He got there by responding to life's temptations instead of to God.

God wants to take us out of the harsh life we're experiencing—the hurt, the pain, the disappointment, the frustration, the distractions—and redeem us. David closed Psalm 19 beautifully with, "Let the words of my mouth and the meditation of my heart be acceptable in your sight, O LORD, my rock and my redeemer" (19:14). When things seem like they're crashing down, when our plans don't work out the way we want them to, God says to us, "I am your rock; I am your redeemer." When we respond to God, He always speaks back into our lives. Like David, we can put faith in God's Word, because He always does what He says He'll do, and He is always right, stable and certain.

David Responds to God's Power

In addition to responding to who God is and to what He has said, we should also respond to His power.

Nature, besides revealing God's beauty, also displays His unfathomable power. Where I live in South Jersey the land is very flat, so we can see a storm coming from miles away. Long before we feel the wind or hear any thunder, we can see streaks of lightning coming down from the sky in the distance. And it's scary and exciting all at the same time. That's just how David describes the power of the Lord in Psalm 29:

>The voice of the LORD is over the waters;
>>the God of glory thunders,
>>the LORD, over many waters. . . .
>The voice of the LORD flashes forth flames of fire. . . .
>The voice of the LORD makes the deer give birth
>>and strips the forests bare,
>>and in his temple all cry, "Glory!" (29:3, 7, 9)

David experienced this storm—he could see the lightning and hear the thunder—and he could see the power of the Lord in the midst of it.

If I saw the storm David described bearing down on me, I'd probably run and hide. And that's okay to do in the storms of life as well—as long as we run to and hide in the right place. When we're faced with disappointment, when we're faced with heartache and sorrow, when we're faced with our own insecurities, where and to whom do we run for protection?

Many times we lose sight of the fact that we serve a powerful God who wants us to respond to Him. We allow the Evil One to keep us in bondage to things like disappointment and fear. Imagine a ton of chains just resting upon our body; if Satan can keep us weighed down like that, then his mission is successful. But God is saying in Psalm 29 that we can break free. All we have to do is claim the power of Christ living in us.

In Psalm 29 the word "Lord" is used eighteen times. David recognizes that he's seeing more than brute nature in the storm; he's seeing a powerful God who can shake the wilderness. This is the same powerful God who wants to shake us out of our sleep and tell us that we don't have to live in fear. We don't have to live in bondage. We don't have to live in response to negative, temporal circumstances. What we need to do is respond to the power of the Lord. This power isn't just for those who are struggling with addictions and shattered lives. Every believer needs the Spirit's presence, and "where the Spirit of the Lord is, there is freedom" (2 Cor. 3:17). Choose to respond to God and to accept His all-encompassing liberty.

How *We* Respond to God

As noted in this book's first chapter, being a man or woman after God's heart involves hearing His call and being anointed for His purpose. But there's an active component there for us—in order to hear and obey God's call, we have to listen for Him, and we have to respond to Him. The real challenge is responding *well*. When life gets crazy and all our relationships feel like they're falling apart, we have to deny our human impulses to get angry and upset and to shut down, and instead we have turn to the Lord.

This isn't particularly easy for me, because I'm the type of person who needs everything to run on a tight, predetermined schedule. I like to be fifteen minutes early for everything, and if I'm not, I get anxious. I'll be in the house chanting, "Let's *go!*" when we have more than enough time not only to get wherever we're going but to get there early. Because of this tendency of mine, I don't always respond to others in the correct way when my schedule is busy, and that hurts my relationship with the Lord.

When my son went to his first day of camp, I wanted to make sure that I was there on time at the end of the day to pick him up. Unfortunately, I had a busy day at the church where I work. I had a packed to-do list—training new people for our media team and helping with several ministries. So by the time I left my office, I was already running late to get my son. I hustled to the church parking lot, only to discover that my car wasn't where I'd left it. Now, I have a healthy, joking relationship with the facilities team. We're always teasing one another and pulling pranks. (Once they made my office look like a barn and set a rooster loose in it, but that's a story for another day.) So naturally, I accused the facilities guys first. I marched into their office and demanded that they tell me where my car was, but they vehemently denied having done anything. "How would we know where your car is?" they asked with a suspicious twinkle in their eyes.

The joking continued for several minutes as I became more and more upset. It was almost past time for me to be at my son's camp, and I hadn't even left the church yet! In total exasperation I stomped down to the other end of the building. And lo and behold, there was my car—not in the parking lot but pulled up onto the concrete walkway, its front bumper almost touching the doors of our welcome center. The logical thing would have been to exit out of another door, but in my anger and frustration, I pushed the door open into my bumper and squeezed through the tiny opening to get to my car. As I backed out and drove away in a huff, I was furious that my schedule—as inconsequential as it may have been—had been disrupted. I can look back now and laugh, but at the time I responded totally incorrectly—getting angry when I should have recognized that the whole thing was in good fun.

Often when something puts a kink in our plan for the day, we don't respond well. Instead of seeking to find God's heart for the situation, we find ourselves negatively responding to the people around us and to our own personal flaws. Rather than turning to the One who is all-sufficient, we allow our insufficiencies to define us. How we react to the various things that happen to us reveal a lot about where we've placed our focus. We find fulfillment when we focus on our Creator.

When God Responds to Our Need

Early in my ministry career I served as a youth pastor. One of the kids in my ministry was a boy named Jesse. Jesse's attendance was intermittent, but it wasn't because he had a weak faith; it was because he was often too sick to come to youth group. He had cancer, and chemotherapy took a lot out of him. Yet Jesse was strong, and his life perspective influenced many around him. Jesse's mom even started coming to church—searching for answers to heavy questions like "God, why are You allowing this to happen to my son? Why is he going through this pain? Why is my marriage on the rocks? Why, why, why?"

On July 10, 2004, Jesse went home to be with the Lord. Jesse's mom was angry and upset. Now she had even more questions, but instead of seeking God, she said, "God, enough is enough. You haven't answered my prayers, so I'm done trying to respond to You. I'm done trying to reach out to You." She almost entirely cut off her relationship with the Lord, but then she shared her feelings of hurt and anger with our pastor's wife, and our pastor's wife very wisely shared, "God is big enough to handle our anger." That new perspective changed everything for her from that point on.

It's true—God is big enough to handle our anger. He is big enough to handle our pain. He is big enough to handle our lives. In Matthew 11:28–30, Jesus says, "Come to me, all who labor and are heavy laden, and I will give you rest. Take my yoke upon you, and learn from me, for I am gentle and lowly in heart, and you will find rest for your souls. For my yoke is easy, and my burden is light." The central command of this passage is to *come*. All we have to do to be relieved of our heavy burdens is to respond to Christ, to bow before Him and ask Him to take all our whys and dark storms and troubles.

We saw in Psalm 19 how David responded to God, but also in the psalm we can see that God was also making Himself accessible to David, since the Lord was speaking through His creation and through His Word. In John 1 we learn how God made Himself accessible to all mankind:

In the beginning was the Word, and the Word was with God, and the Word was God. He was in the beginning with God.

All things were made through him, and without him was not
any thing made that was made. In him was life, and the life
was the light of men. The light shines in the darkness, and the
darkness has not overcome it. . . . And the Word became flesh
and dwelt among us. (1:1–5, 14)

Jesus came to earth so that we would no longer have to
respond to the hurts of this life but could instead respond to
God's grace. We no longer have to live in bondage to anger, fear,
sin or whatever is plaguing us. When Christ shed His blood, He
opened the door for us to respond to God's being and power, to
draw near to Him. The Lord wants to give us strength. He wants
to bless us with His presence. He wants us to live victoriously, no
longer responding to life but to Him.

How will we respond?

Let's Pray:

*Father God, I come to You, asking You to show me how
to respond to Your Spirit. Lord, I ask that Your anointing
would fall on me and that You would speak clearly to my
heart. I pray in Jesus' name, amen.*

CHAPTER THREE

DAVID, A MAN AFTER GOD'S OWN HEART: CHOOSING TO OBEY

1 Samuel 13–16

Pastor Glenn Kantner

*But Samuel replied, "What is more pleasing to the LORD: your burnt
offerings and sacrifices or your obedience to his voice?
Listen! Obedience is better than sacrifice, and submission
is better than offering the fat of rams."*
1 Samuel 15:22

Responding to God in the right ways requires obedience, and that's not easy for us naturally rebellious types. It's one thing to know what we're *supposed* to do, but it's something entirely different to obey what we've been commanded to do. God doesn't leave us in the dark as to what He wants from us; He doesn't hide from us how to be "after His heart."

The Bible is peppered with verses urging obedience: "Be careful to do according to all the law . . . that you may have good success wherever you go" (Josh. 1:7). "Keep the charge of the LORD your God, walking in his ways and keeping his statutes, his commandments, his rules, and his testimonies . . . that you may prosper in all that you do and wherever you turn" (1 Kings 2:3). "Delight yourself in the LORD, and he will give you the desires of your heart" (Ps. 37:4). "Hezekiah sought "his God, he did with all his heart, and prospered" (2 Chron. 31:21).

Being obedient isn't always about following a checklist or doing what feels most natural to us. In fact, most of the time it involves ignoring what we think we know and *choosing* to follow what God is saying instead. Obedience requires active submission to God. Being "after God's heart" means having to give up a little of our own heart in the process. While the correct decision to make isn't always clear-cut, the key to obeying God is never to lose the desire to honor and glorify God through our choices.

When we make a decision, we reveal what's in our heart. Are our hearts clean and eager to serve the Lord, or are they dark and bitter? In this chapter we're going to step back chronologically, to before David's anointing, and compare and contrast the lives of King Saul and David. And, I hope, we will honestly evaluate the condition of our own hearts. The state of our hearts dictates far more of our decisions and reactions to life than we might realize. So what does it look like, spiritually speaking, to have a good heart?

David: Good Hearts Trust God

One of the surefire ways to have a healthy heart is to trust God. The Lord will never lead us astray, and when our hearts rest in Him and are focused on His ways, we're protected from making bad decisions. Trusting in the Lord, however, is not a once-time activity. We have to continually recommit ourselves to following Him, or we can slip back into sinful decision-making patterns. King Saul offers us a tragic example of what happens when we stop trusting God in *all* things.

King Saul had been king for only a short time when his son, Jonathan, successfully conquered a garrison of Philistines. The book of first Samuel tells us the Philistines responded by amassing a huge army to fight back: "The Philistines mustered to fight Israel, thirty thousand chariots and six thousand horsemen and troops like the sand on the seashore in multitude" (13:5). Saul had maybe three thousand men at best, and the Philistine army had cut off any hope he had of getting reinforcements from the north. So, vastly outnumbered, the Israelites ran and hid.

Even though Saul's army was melting away like butter, he had been commanded by Samuel to wait seven days for the prophet to come offer a sacrifice and to get a word from God as to how the Israelites were to proceed. Saul waited, but by the end of the seven-day period, Samuel still hadn't shown.

Saul tired of waiting for Samuel and decided to offer the sacrifice himself. But just as he finished, Samuel showed up and demanded, "What have you done? . . . You have done foolishly . . . You have not kept the command of the LORD your God, with which he commanded you. For then the LORD would have established your kingdom over Israel forever. But now your kingdom shall not continue. The LORD has sought out a man after his own heart, and the LORD has commanded him to be prince over his people, because you have not kept what the LORD commanded you" (13:11, 13–14).

Saul had found himself in some difficult circumstances: His army was scattering. The Philistines were just about ready to attack. But instead of standing fast in what Samuel had told him to do, Saul reasoned to himself, "The Philistines will come down against me at Gilgal, and I have not sought the favor of the LORD" (13:12). Saul's thought appears to be a good one. He did not want to go into battle without having sought the Lord. It almost sounds like his heart was in the right place. But subsequent events proved that it was not. You see, God had told him ahead of time not to do anything until Samuel arrived. Certainly God knew Saul's circumstances. But rather than obey, Saul allowed his circumstances to breed fear in his heart, which led to disobedience. Saul said, "So I forced myself, and offered the burnt offering" (13:12).

Notice the three steps:

Threatening circumstances → fear → compulsive disobedience

We've all been tempted to follow these steps. We hit the point of needing relief from some situation or difficult circumstance, and we sacrifice something important to get that relief. When we feel lonely, we might take the first guy or gal who comes along just so we can have companionship. When we struggle financially, we might go ahead with a shady business transaction just to get money. When we're concerned about our reputation, we might compromise our values to be accepted by those around us. Fears—of being alone, of being impoverished, of being rejected—all types of fears can cause us to act on impulse and to take matters into our own hands, often with disastrous results.

Compare King Saul's actions to David's. First Samuel 16 tells us that David was a brave man and a warrior (see 16:18). Scripture tells us that David fought lions and bears with his bare hands to protect his flock (see 17:34–35). David was not a fearful person, because he relied on the Lord through scary circumstances:

> When I am afraid,
>   I put my trust in you.
> In God, whose word I praise,
>   in God I trust; I shall not be afraid.
>   What can flesh do to me? (56:3–4)

It's worth noting that David wrote that psalm when he was in a Philistine prison (see chapter description of Ps. 56). He had no idea what the Philistines might do to him; as far as he know, they might kill him. But instead of being afraid, David sought after God's heart of peace and placed his total trust in the Lord.

It's natural to feel anxious from time to time, but fear has a way of taking over our lives and ruling the decisions we make. When we get worried about getting old or not having enough money or wrecking a relationship, we need to claim the Lord's peace over our situation. Fear will cloud our decision-making and rob us of the joy of the Lord. Like David did, we need to have a heart that trusts God—even when we're facing something that scares us.

David: Good Hearts Are Humble

"Heart problems" aren't always obvious sins like lying or cheating or ignoring God's Word. Being proud of what we've done is just as detrimental to our walk with the Lord, because God is the one who deserves all the credit for drawing us to Himself. David never reveled in self-glorification; he wasn't prideful. From him we learn that good hearts are humble. Unfortunately, this was a lesson Saul learned the hard way.

Remember the huge army that had trapped King Saul and his men? Well, while Saul was panicking, his son Jonathan and his armor bearer sneaked up to a Philistine lookout post and killed about twenty men. When word of this infiltration reached the Philistines' main camp, God shook the ground (see 14:15). The Philistines, now without their lookouts, may have thought the shaking earth was caused by a huge Israelite army approaching. They panicked and began to swing their swords at anyone near them—including each other.

Hearing of the chaos at the Philistine camp, Saul gathered his men and gave chase. But then he made a critical decision that put Jonathan at great risk: "The men of Israel had been hard pressed that day, so Saul had laid an oath on the people, saying, 'Cursed be the man who eats food until it is evening and I am avenged on my enemies'" (14:24). Saul wanted to appear zealous and firm, like a leader in complete control who would lead his men to conquer the Philistines once and for all. Instead, he made a decision that nearly cost the life of his son. That's because Jonathan had been away when Saul had made his pronouncement, winning the battle against the Philistines, so he didn't hear Saul's declaration. Jonathan ate, and Saul was forced to abide by his oath. By God's grace, however, Saul's army came between the two men and said, in so many words, "We can't kill Jonathan. He's the reason we have victory" (see 14:45). Saul backed down, but in doing so, he lost face in front of his men.

Why would Saul make a decision that not only hurt his reputation but could also have made him kill his own offspring? It was due to pride. Saul wanted to appear decisive and in control— so much so that he was willing to kill his son to defend his title. Scripture makes it clear that Saul was an exceedingly proud king. Even though it was Jonathan, not King Saul, who had defeated the Philistines, First Samuel 13:4 reports, "All Israel heard it said that Saul had defeated the garrison of the Philistines". Saul then built a monument to his own honor (see 15:12).

Pride is spiritual adultery—stealing the honor and worship that God deserves and keeping it for ourselves. If we have pride in our hearts, our prayers will be self-centered. Pride even affects how we see God. When we place ourselves on a pedestal, we start believing (if subconsciously) that we *deserve* special treatment and recognition. We try to make God into our personal waiter, a "divine vending machine" into which we insert prayer demands and expect to get positive answers in return. Pride also affects our ability to make good decisions, because it teaches us to put ourselves first in every equation.

Thankfully, Scripture provides the antidote to pride: "Cleanse your hands, you sinners, and purify your hearts, you double-minded. . . . Humble yourselves before the Lord, and he will exalt you" (James 4:8, 10). James tells us to confess our sins, seek forgiveness and then submit to God. Admitting that we're all sinners levels the playing field so we don't think of ourselves as better than anyone else, and remembering who God is humbles us to remember our place.

Unlike Saul, David seemed to understand this. He lived

humbly. For example, when he was anointed by Samuel to become the next king of Israel, David didn't build a statue of himself; he went back to being a shepherd (see 1 Sam. 16:19). The Psalms are filled with David's admissions that he couldn't succeed without the Lord's help and power.

Saul could have behaved the same way. He could have glorified God instead of seeking praise for himself, and he could have waited on God instead of fearfully and arrogantly trying to control his situation on his own. But because Saul persisted in his pride, lack of faith and fear, he ended up losing his kingship and ultimately his life (read First Samuel 15–31 for the full story). I can't help but think that David must have been recalling Saul's downfall when he wrote,

> Love the LORD, all you his saints!
> > The LORD preserves the faithful
> > but abundantly repays the one who acts in pride. (Ps. 31:23)

The first step in making a good decision is moving past our pride to humble our heart before the Lord. Otherwise, we'll end up like proud Saul—bitter, rejected and powerless. Humility may seem difficult to accept, but remember, we're never stronger than when we're fully submitted to the Lord!

David: Good Hearts are Obedient

Humility gives us a better understanding of who we are in light of who God is. When we have a right perspective of the Lord, we realize that He knows what is best for us, which leads to a desire on our part to obey Him. I'm not saying that it's always easy to obey; we're naturally rebellious, so every act of obedience requires effort. But training our hearts to trust the Lord and to be humble before Him makes it easier for us to obey His Word.

Once again, Saul gives us an example of a heart set on self-aggrandizement rather than on God's heart. Saul struggled with being obedient. In First Samuel 15 he was commanded by God to eliminate the Amalekites, an evil people who opposed the Israelites' liberation from Egypt. God made it clear that Saul was to destroy the entire city of Amalek—all the people, all their animals, everything. Saul did attack the city, but he didn't fully obey God's instructions: "Saul and the people spared Agag and the best of the sheep and of the oxen and of the fattened calves and the lambs, and all that was good, and would not utterly destroy them. All that was despised and worthless they devoted to destruction" (15:9).

Saul not only intentionally disobeyed the Lord's command; he also lied about it when confronted by Samuel, saying, "I have performed the commandment of the LORD" (15:13). Samuel, however, was no fool. He noted the bleating of sheep and the lowing of cattle. Samuel knew he wouldn't be hearing any animals if Saul had actually done what the Lord had commanded him to do. Evidence proving Saul's guilt was all around him.

Saul's response was to rationalize his disobedience: "'I have obeyed the voice of the LORD,' Saul said. 'I have gone on the mission on which the LORD sent me. I have brought Agag the king of Amalek, and I have devoted the Amalekites to destruction. But the people took of the spoil, sheep and oxen, the best of the things devoted to destruction, to sacrifice to the Lord your God in Gilgal'" (15:20–21). Saul tried to twist what he had done into something positive; he tried to justify his actions by claiming that giving a sacrifice to the Lord was actually better than following God's instructions. Dangerous thinking!

When we live in disobedience, we find that we can rationalize anything to suit our own selfish interests. Saul made a bad decision because his heart followed his own desires rather than God's. Samuel reminded Saul of his place, sarcastically asking, "Has the LORD as great delight in burnt offerings and sacrifices, as in obeying the voice of the LORD? Behold, to obey is better than sacrifice, and to listen than the fat of rams" (15:22).

Obedience is one of the central things the Lord requires of us, and He delights in us when we follow His teachings.

Consider David. David understood the importance of respectfully submitting to authorities. He obeyed everyone God placed over him. When he was tending sheep, he was obedient to his father. When he went into Saul's service—to play the harp and later to be Saul's armor bearer—David obeyed Saul without question, finding favor with the king in the process (see 16:22). Psalm 119 gives us yet another insight into the obedience of David's heart: "I hold back my feet from every evil way, in order to keep your word" (119:101).

Because of David's servant heart, he was favored by the Lord and by the people above him. Because David was trustworthy and obedient, Saul eventually made him the commander of over one thousand men! Obedience to God, while challenging at times, always pays off.

Decisions, Decisions

Kids are great examples of people's natural propensity to choose wrong. One day I was at my daughter's house, and she and I were watching her boys play. My grandson Jack was occupying himself with his toys, but my other grandson, Tyler, who was three at the time, kept poking and nudging Jack. For whatever reason, Tyler was dead set on getting on Jack's nerves. Finally my daughter looked over and said, "Tyler, stop bothering your brother." Even though he was only three, Tyler had to make his own decision: would he obey his mother, or would he keep pestering Jack? I watched him think it over. Then he went right up to Jack, put his pointed finger just as close as he could get without touching him, looked impishly back at his mother and said, "Poke." Tyler chose wrongly.

As we get older, the right choice isn't always as obvious to us as it should have been to Tyler. I once co-hosted a small-group study on the book *Building Up One Another* by Dr. Gene Getz. The book focuses on the "one another" passages in the New Testament—passages such as "love one another" (John 13:34), "encourage one another" (1 Thess. 5:11) and "welcome one another" (Rom. 15:7), to name a few.

One night the discussion topic was the Lord's command to "love one another," and I noticed that one of our members, Rob, was unusually quiet, especially as we talked about how loving one another includes loving our enemies and those who aren't easy to love. Eventually Rob opened up and told us about a particular woman he couldn't stand. His dislike was so extreme that he said he wanted to run the other way when he saw her coming! "But," Rob said, "God's telling me to love this woman, and I'm telling you, if I'm going to do this, it's going to have to be God, because I can't do it on my own." We ended the meeting by praying for God to change Rob's heart toward the woman.

The next week Rob shared that he had been at a soccer game the previous Tuesday, and when he had gotten up to leave, he had turned around and found himself face to face with the woman. Rob said that he hadn't known what to do at first, but since he couldn't just act like he hadn't seen the woman and walk away, he decided to put the "love one another" passage into action. Rob greeted her warmly and gave her a big hug. The two of them got to talking, and Rob's church activities came up in the conversation. The woman ended up coming to our church and participating in our Alpha ministry (a course introducing the Christian faith).

Rob obeyed God's command to "love one another," and God honored his sacrifice. That's the same kind of obedience David had. When we obey the way these two men did, we grow into God's best for us.

From our childhood until our dying day, we're faced with

thousands of decisions. And the thing about decisions is that they tell us far more about ourselves—the real us—than we realize. Decisions are like brushstrokes—they paint a portrait of who we are. They show us where we place value, and they reveal our likes and dislikes. Sometimes we'd like to say that reason *forced* us to make a certain choice, but the truth is, what we feel in our hearts is what really makes our choices.

Casting Our Cares

When my grandson Jack was five, he went through a period of ending up in mom and dad's bed every night because he was afraid of the shadows on his wall at night. My daughter mentioned the situation to Jack's pediatrician, and the doctor came up with an idea. "Jack," she told my grandson, "I'm going to write your mother a prescription for some magic water, and she's going to put that magic water in a spray bottle. Whenever you wake up at night feeling scared, just spray the magic water, and it will make all the bad things go away." Jack was excited to try using the magic water that night. But as we might expect, Jack still ended up in his parents' bedroom. He said, "Mom, I don't think that magic water works." Jack was right; "magic water" wasn't going to solve his problem or alleviate his fear.

We're more like Jack than we might want to admit. We get fearful and anxious from time to time—sometimes without much reason. We all have our own "magic water" that we use to try to handle difficult circumstances and challenges. To make ourselves feel better or to distract ourselves from our worries, some of us eat comfort food, some of us go shopping, and some of us even turn to drugs, alcohol or sex. But none of these things ever fixes the problem; it only masks it or intensifies it until we find ourselves scared and searching for the next fix. No "magic water"—no substance or person or experience—can change the heart. But the Lord can.

Jack's mom and dad decided to take different approach. They helped Jack memorize First Peter 5:7—"Cast all your anxiety on him because he cares for you"—and told him to repeat that verse to himself the next time he felt afraid in the middle of the night. They helped Jack understand that God is with him at all times. They taught Jack Bible stories, like the one about how God sent his angel to protect Daniel in the lions' den. They prayed with Jack so he wouldn't feel so anxious, and they reminded him of how God had been faithful to deliver him from his fears in the past. And guess what? It worked. Jack was freed from his fear and started sleeping in his own room.

Like Jack, when we have a heart that trusts in the Lord and in His promises, we're freed from anxiety and can make decisions that are truly good.

Test Yourself

None of us always make perfect decisions, but when we seek to have trusting, humble, obedient hearts, we get closer to God. In turn, He honors our commitment and enables us to obey better and better and to know Him more and more. It's important to be aware of how we make decisions. We need to ask ourselves: Have I made decisions primarily out of fear, or does the way I live my life reflect total trust in God's will and design for my life? Do I often try to make myself look good and superior to others (pride), or have I sought to humble myself before other people and God? Do I tend to obey my own desires (whatever feels easiest or most personally fulfilling in a situation), or do I strive to put God's Word first, being more concerned with honoring Him than with comforting myself?

This exercise isn't meant to make us feel guilty, but it should make us question where our priorities lie and where our hearts are. When our decisions reflect that our hearts are far from God, we need to pray that the Holy Spirit will show us how to grow closer to Him. (This might involve accepting Jesus Christ as Savior and Lord for the first time. This is the best decision a person can ever make, and it's certainly the one we need to start with to see change for the better in our hearts.)

Those who have already asked Jesus to be their Lord and Savior would benefit from getting into a small-group Bible study or other fellowship group where people will love them and help them grow in the areas in which they're struggling. God wants us to be in community with other believers so we can challenge and strengthen one another, encouraging each other to trust God more and to humbly obey Him!

We have to make the choice to develop a heart that refuses fear and chooses to trust in God. We need to deny our pride and seek to develop a humble heart that obeys God's commands.

Let's Pray:

Help us, Lord, to be like David—to choose to follow You and to seek Your heart—instead of having our hearts in the wrong place, as Saul did, and making bad decisions. Let it be so!

CHAPTER FOUR

DAVID AND GOLIATH:
BEATING LIFE'S GIANT PROBLEMS

1 Samuel 17

Pastor Marty Berglund

*You come to me with a sword and with a spear and with a javelin,
but I come to you in the name of the LORD of hosts, the God of the
armies of Israel, whom you have defied.*
1 Samuel 17:45

God intends for us to have great victories, yet we too often get trapped under heavy burdens and in losing battles. Difficulties suffocate us, and no matter how hard we try, we can't seem to overcome them. Part of being victorious involves accepting that we're *never* going to be able to win battles on our own. God-sized problems require God-sized aid. The Lord wants to protect our hearts to keep us from fear. I pray the Holy Spirit will illuminate the story of David and Goliath to us so that we can see its relevance for our lives and our situations.

David's Battle

The tale of David and Goliath is one of the most popular stories in human history. This episode of a little servant boy taking down a mighty warrior was hugely significant. The story of David and Goliath is not just some felt-board story for a

Sunday school teacher; it should have a potent impact on all our lives. David's courage and his victory were both matters of his heart, not his actual physical strength. David took a step of faith and relied on God to see him through, and God blessed him because of it.

First Samuel 17 starts out setting the stage for a battle. The armies of Philistia and Israel had met at the Valley of Elah. Picture it. The Philistines were on one hill, the Israelites were on another, and the air was tense as they waited to battle. And then there was a game-changer: "And there came out from the camp of the Philistines a champion named Goliath of Gath, whose height was six cubits and a span" (17:4). The National Basketball Association would have loved Goliath, because he was about nine feet, nine inches tall. Verse 5 tells us that Goliath was wearing a bronze helmet and a coat of mail that weighed 5,000 shekels of bronze, which is about 125 pounds. In addition. he had bronze armor covering his legs and a bronze javelin with an iron spearhead weighing 600 shekels, which is about fifteen to twenty pounds. That guy had to have been huge to be able to carry and wield all that weight!

Goliath marched into the valley and shouted to the ranks of Israel:

> Why have you come out to draw up for battle? Am I not a Philistine, and are you not servants of Saul? Choose a man for yourselves, and let him come down to me. If he is able to fight with me and kill me, then we will be your servants. But if I prevail against him and kill him, then you shall be our servants and serve us. . . . I defy the ranks of Israel this day. Give me a man, that we may fight together. (17:8–11)

So one big guy was standing there defying all Israel, saying, "Who do you think you are, coming out to fight us? Send someone out to fight me, and if I can't beat the guy, then we'll all be your servants. But if I win, then you have to be our servants.

Come on and fight!" Goliath set up a battle of representation. Rather than have thousands of people die, why not just have one guy fight one guy? Sounds like a pretty reasonable idea—except in this case it meant someone from Israel had to fight a giant, which would have been pretty nerve-racking. The Israelites were discouraged and frightened.

Then First Samuel abruptly switches from talking about the mounting battle to telling us about David, a lowly shepherd boy out tending his flock. Talk about a total one-eighty from the war scene! Anyway, David's dad, Jesse, called David in from the field and said, "Hey, Dave, I want you to go to where the soldiers are camped and see how your brothers are doing." Jesse's three oldest sons were fighting for the Israelites. "Here's a bushel of food and some cheese for the commander. Bring a message back to me."

When David got to the battle line, the men of Israel asked him, "Have you seen this man [Goliath] who has come up? Surely he has come up to defy Israel. And the king will give enrich the man who kills him with great riches and will give him his daughter and will make his father's house free in Israel" (17:25). David considered all this—not having to pay taxes, marrying a princess, honoring his family—and he asked, "Who is this uncircumcised Philistine, that he should defy the armies of the living God?" (17:26).

Saul heard that David was asking questions, and he sent for him. David said to Saul, "Let no man's heart fail because of him. Your servant will go and fight this Philistine" (17:32). Saul probably had a good chuckle. A shepherd boy was standing in front of him boldly asserting that he would go fight a giant! "You are not able to go against this Philistine to fight with him, for you are but a youth, and he has been a man of war from his youth," Saul told David (17:33). But David would not be turned away.

He told Saul how he had wrestled with and killed lions and bears to protect his flock, and he asserted, "This uncircumcised Philistine shall be like one of them, for he has defied the armies of the living God" (17:36). So Saul caved: "Yeah, okay. Go. The Lord be with you."

What a chicken Saul was! If anybody was going to fight Goliath, it should have been Saul. He was the guy in charge! He was the king! But he was afraid, so he clothed David in his armor and sent him out to fight in his place. David, however, was just a little guy, so he couldn't even walk in Saul's armor. He took the armor off, picked up his staff and chose five smooth stones from the brook, which he put in his shepherd's pouch.

David, armed with no more than a sling and five stones (and his trust in the Lord), went to face the Philistine champion clad in hundreds of pounds of armor. That had to be a sight to see! Scripture quotes some of Goliath's trash talk for us. The Philistine mocked, "Am I a dog, that you come to me with sticks? . . . Come to me, and I will give your flesh to the birds of the air and to the beasts of the field" (17:43–44).

David trash-talks right back:

> You come to me with a sword and with a spear and with a javelin, but I come against you in the name of the Lord of hosts, the God of the armies of Israel, whom you have defied. This day the Lord will deliver you into my hand, and I will strike you down and cut off your head. And I will give the dead bodies of the host of the Philistines this day to the birds of the air and to the wild beasts of the earth, that all the earth may know that there is a God in Israel. (17:45–46)

David got a little sassy, but his heart never altered from its purpose—to make God known and to honor His name. Goliath, incensed by David's insults, moved closer to attack. And David ran at him. *He ran toward a giant.* David grabbed a stone out of his bag, slung it at the Philistine, hit him right in the forehead and knocked him out. Then David grabbed the Philistine's sword, killed him and cut off his head. And just like that, the battle was decided.

When the rest of the Philistines saw that their champion had lost, they fled. The men of Israel and Judah pursued the Philistines as far as Gath, and, well, it got pretty gruesome. (I won't get into those details.) The story of David and Goliath seems like the classic underdog story, but David wasn't actually at a disadvantage, because God was with him. David relied on the Lord's strength rather than his own to win the battle and to defend Israel, and that's why he succeeded.

Step One: Stop Looking at the Giant

We all have giants in our lives. Maybe our giant is a medical problem—cancer or heart disease or diabetes. Maybe our giant is the death of something or someone—our spouse or a close friend or a life dream. Or maybe our giant is an emotional issue—depression or a broken heart or a feeling of inadequacy. At some point, everyone has struggled with a huge, seemingly insurmountable problem.

Remember in the story when the Israelites were trembling before Goliath? Why were they afraid? Why wouldn't any of them fight? They were all looking at Goliath, and he looked big and threatening.

Just like the Israelites, sometimes all we can see is our problem. We can't get past the pain we're feeling or our doctor's diagnosis or what our friends are telling us. I'm not dismissing specialists who help us pinpoint problems or friends who speak truth into our lives. But sometimes all we seem to look at is what's wrong with our lives. If you're afraid or nervous or anxious, I can guarantee you that you're looking at the wrong thing. Just like the Israelites, you're focusing on your giant, and it's ruining your perspective on the situation.

Verse 25 of First Samuel 17 says that the men of Israel were questioning, "Have you seen this man who has come up?" Notice the words "has come up," indicating that as Goliath mocked

Israel, he walked across the valley and started coming up their hill. And the men of Israel were terrified by it.

That's what happens with our giants as well. They intimidate us, and we fixate on them. In our fear, the giants grow—they get closer and more real. The next thing we know, our giant is entirely dominating our thought life. It's controlling everything we do, and it has us so anxious that we're taking medication just to find some relief. Here's our problem: we're looking at the giant.

I know it's difficult in the midst of a problem—when the giant's right there staring us down—to refocus our attention. But somehow we have to get our hearts and minds off the things that make us anxious, because it's the plan of the Enemy to distract us from all things good and noble and pure.

Both cowards and heroes get afraid, and both of them run, but one runs the wrong way, and the other runs the right way. Sure, we're going to be afraid. But the question is, what are we going to do with our fear?

Step Two: Get Out of the Way

Who or what is the biggest giant a person could possibly face? The loss of a child or a job? A disease? An impossible relationship? I would suggest that none of these is the answer. In fact, I would say that the biggest giant of every one of us is the same thing, and it's not a disease or a problem or a person—it's ourselves.

The truth is that it's not what the doctor tells us; it's how we respond. It's not what our spouse does to us; it's how we react. It's not what our enemy asks us; it's how we reply. The problem is us—we're our own Goliaths. The Bible calls this giant our old self, our sinful nature. We hurt ourselves the most when we allow our inadequacies and worries to control us. And until we fight that Goliath, everything else is secondary. That's why Jesus said, "If anyone would come after me, let him deny himself and take up his cross and follow me" (Matt. 16:24). The apostle Paul wrote about dying to self (see Gal. 2:20). If we want victory over our giant, our self, we have to deny our own desires and fears and live for Christ.

Several years back we had a strong Christian couple that was highly involved in our church. They had a tremendous effect on others' lives, but their marriage was falling apart. They went to counseling sessions, but after awhile it became obvious that they weren't really seeking help. All the husband could do was talk about his wife and blame her. And all she could see was what was wrong with him. We couldn't get them to fight the real giant, which was themselves. If for just a few moments they would have reflected on their own giants—like pride, selfishness, greed and lust—maybe there could have been healing and reconciliation. But instead, after thirty-some years of marriage, they got divorced. It was devastating.

The weapons of the Enemy are subtle and ingrained deeply within us. The devil spurs us to selfishness and anger when we should be focused on serving others and loving them. Satan's javelins and spears are fear, envy, insecurity, bitterness, despair.

Once I met a guy from my church for lunch. When I asked him how things were going, he said, "I've lost everything—my money, the house, everything. It's over, man. I'm done for." I sat there for a few minutes thinking about what he was saying.

I looked him in the eyes and asked, "Do you still have the Lord? Is He still your Savior?"

"Yeah, of course," he quickly replied.

"Do you still have your wife, whom you deeply love?"

"Yes."

"Do you still have your precious children?" He nodded. I continued, "You just told me that you still have the three most important things in your life—the Lord, your wife and your kids. Yet you're telling me you've lost everything. I don't think so. You lost some money. You lost a house. Big deal."

I knew I was being bold to say that to him, and I wasn't trying to discount his loss; I just wanted him to see the real problem. He was focused on the wrong thing. Whenever I see him now, he thanks me for that reality check, for speaking truth into his situation.

It's much easier to point out how others are focusing on the wrong things than it is to honestly evaluate how we're defeating ourselves. It's a serious challenge to admit that we're getting in the way of the Lord's best for us. Ironically, the best way to see how we've fallen short isn't to focus on our shortcomings. Instead, we have to set our sights on the ultimate standard of perfection: the Lord.

Step Three: Stay Focused on God

If we want to have victory, we have to stop looking at our giants. When we focus on the Lord, He gives us a proper perspective, and our giants shrink in comparison to His power and goodness.

Consider the difference between the Israelite soldiers' responses to the Philistine and David's response. The Israelites quaked before Goliath, but David was indignant: "Who does this guy think he is, challenging God's people like this? We can't allow him to mock our Lord like this!" When even the mightiest warriors that Israel had to offer were cowering, this punk kid was declaring, "Let me fight! I can beat this guy, because the Lord is with me." David remembered that the Lord could do anything.

Do we see the truth in there? Sometimes we might not want to fight, but it's not about whether or not we have energy or strength or we feel like it, because winning isn't up to us. Our problems might be big—huge, even—but the Lord is bigger than *anything* we might face.

As I mentioned earlier, Saul should have been the one to face Goliath. Saul was taller and bigger and more powerful than any of the other Israelites. God had anointed Saul king, but Saul had forgotten God. Saul didn't search the Scriptures for truth or motivation. He didn't talk to the prophets. And because he wasn't focused on God, Saul nearly missed out on God's power to win the battle. The Israelites too tried to play it safe by refusing to fight, but their fear and insecurity were actually more damaging to them than any battle could have been.

The giants in our lives cause us to forget what we need to remember and to remember what we should be forgetting. We need to remember that we're children of God and that God is going to work through us. When Christ lives in us, we share in His power and authority (see Matt. 28:18–20). But too often we forget that we are God's chosen and sanctified people. Instead, all we think is, *I really blew it back there!* or, *I don't feel so good*, or, *Ugh! That person is impossible.*

If we as Christians—redeemed people, the chosen children of God—don't stay close to God through reading the Word, praying and fellowshipping with Him, we make ourselves susceptible to giants. And giants so shake our world that they pull our attention away from what matters most—loving God and loving others (see Matt. 22:37–39).

When we're not directly facing a battle, we should be in preparation—getting our hearts right with God. That way, when a giant comes onto the scene, we're ready. It's important to spend time with the Lord, to go to church, to be in community and to get involved in small prayer groups. We don't want to spend our days trembling and being anxious; we want to be prepared to declare the Lord's victory over every battle!

Step Four: Recognize that the Battle Belongs to the Lord

Maybe, like the Israelites, we're questioning God, "Why are

You letting this happen?" We need to shift our perspective—to ask, like David, "What is this problem that it should cause me to question God? Do I not believe that He loves me and is great enough to defend and save me?" The battle is the Lord's. I'm not saying that He caused it, but I am saying that He is the key to victory. Christians' first line of defense is the Lord; we need to remember Him when life feels too intimidating to fight.

David had God plus nothing, so he won the battle. It's the same with us against the giants in our lives, including the giant of our sinful nature. God brought the Philistine before Israel to (re) teach them the lesson that He and He alone—with no additions or subtractions—could bring them through any situation. God allows giants in our lives to teach us the same lesson. All we need to win the battle is Jesus, and Jesus alone.

David went into battle without a spear or a sword or a shield, which tells me we don't need to worry if we don't feel properly equipped to fight. We need to stop making excuses for inaction— saying that we're too weak or too tired or too overwhelmed. I'll say it again: *the battle is the Lord's*. We just have to be willing to fight. No doctor, lawyer, pastor, teacher, friend, government or spouse can fight for us; we have to face our own battle and say, "I'm in, Lord. My problem still looks huge to me, and I can't do this on my own, but I'm trusting You to bring victory."

I highly recommend the book *Brokenness: How God Redeems Pain and Suffering* by Lon Solomon. In it Solomon says that we have a natural, built-in resistance to God. He traces through Scripture how God uses pain and suffering to break up the giants that control us. One of the parts of the book that I found the most moving was Solomon's story of his daughter Jill's birth. Right after she was born, she went into convulsions, and the family struggled to care for the baby because of her persistent sickness. At the time Solomon's church in Washington, DC, had grown and was thriving, and he asked the Lord why He would allow this all-consuming challenge to enter his family's life. *How is this going to prosper Your kingdom?* Solomon questioned. *Why are You doing this to us?*

Jill's convulsions continued for years as Solomon searched his heart to see if there was some way in which he was being defiantly sinful. He said he tried to control everything and to fix the situation, demanding that God perform a miracle to heal his daughter. His prayers didn't seem to change anything. Solomon writes, "I finally reached a place where I had to release Jill and her health into the hands of God; to surrender her and turn it loose. I felt a lot like Abraham in Genesis chapter 22, when God asked Abraham to sacrifice his son on the altar. Finally I was done."[1]

When Solomon finally surrendered to the Lord, God turned everything around. Jill regained her mobility, and Solomon writes, "[My wife] Brenda and I felt hope seeping back into our lives." Solomon's preaching was empowered, and he had a new heart for the people of his congregation. His church grew by leaps and bounds. "Here's the point," he said. "God had done a work of brokenness in my life. Removing the resistance to Him—as small as I thought it was, He had knocked every human prop out from under me. He had smashed my self-sufficiency. He had smashed my self-wisdom. He had smashed my self-resourcefulness. He reduced me to Jesus plus nothing."

Step Five: Face the Battle

Now is the time to turn our problems over to the Lord. It's our choice: will we stop focusing on everything that's wrong and start looking at the Lord?

I know that's easier said than done, so I want to give a few pointers to help us turn our battles over to the Lord. First, get into the Word. Ephesians 6:17 tells us the Bible is the "sword of the Spirit." If we're going into battle, we need to be built up and strong in our faith. We need to know God's truth for our situation, and the best way to hear from Him is through His Word! Second, we need to pray. Don't think of this as thirty minutes of quiet time to check off a list. Through the power of the Holy Spirit, we can converse with the Lord of lords, who knows what we need in order to win our battle before we ever even ask. Prayer is powerful! And third, we need to be in a small group with other believers that meets regularly. The whole point of community is for believers to build one another up and to encourage one another through difficult times. When we start looking at our giants, others can help us turn our heart and mind back to God.

When we declare that we're broken inside—that we have sinned and messed up and don't know where to turn—but that the battle is the Lord's, He will fight for us and will renew us from the inside out. We need to stop focusing on everything that's wrong. We need to admit to the Lord that our giant is too big to handle. We need to tell Him we believe that He is our first line of defense in our battle and that we're going to start praying and living as if we believe it. And then, in the name of Jesus, we need to accept God's freedom from our giants!

Let's Pray:

Father, give us the strength to face life's giants, knowing that You go before us to clear the way for our victory. The battle is certainly Yours. Thank You for setting us free to focus on You. In Jesus' name, amen.

CHAPTER FIVE

DAVID'S RISE TO KINGSHIP: THE KEY TO REAL SUCCESS

1 Samuel 18

Pastor Glenn Kantner

And David had success in all his undertakings,
for the LORD was with him.
1 Samuel 18:14

The idea of success in America often conjures up images of monetary extravagance and luxury. A few years ago Dennis Koslowski, former CEO of Tyco International, threw a birthday bash for his wife, Karen. This week-long party was held in Sardinia, just off the coast of Italy, and it cost over two million dollars. It was quite the shindig. When guests arrived, young women dressed in togas and jewel-laden headdresses threw rose petals at their feet. Jimmy Buffet performed, and there was a laser-light show. Koslowski even had an ice sculpture of Michelangelo's David made that doubled as a fountain and gushed expensive vodka.

Pretty interesting. Dennis could afford this party because at that time in his life, he was making just under two hundred million dollars a year. Most of us would look at someone like Dennis and say, "Wow, that guy was pretty successful." Only problem is that he ended up in jail a couple of years later on charges of improperly appropriating company funds. Would we call that successful? And if not, what is success, and how do we get it?

I think the real question we need to ask is this: how do we become successful in accordance with what Scripture teaches and in a way that's beneficial? Sometimes it's difficult for us to see the distinction between worldly success and spiritual success, but we need to evaluate whether we're just keeping up appearances or truly living in a way that honors the Lord. David kept his heart focused on glorifying the Lord, not himself, and we need to do the same. Let's examine how.

A David Kind of Success

Because David wholeheartedly trusted the Lord, God blessed him and allowed him to prosper. David didn't seek success or glory—he sought to make God known, and God honored David's heart. David's life demonstrates the key to success—and it doesn't look anything like what this world has to offer.

First Samuel 18 offers us good examples of success and failure. We've been tracking David's successes over the past couple of chapters, and in chapter 18 we learn that people around David were aware of his abilities, dedication and trustworthiness: "David went out and was successful wherever Saul sent him, so that Saul set him over the men of war. And this was good in the sight of all the people and also in the sight of Saul's servants" (18:5). When David returned from slaying the Philistine, women came out of all the cities of Israel, dancing and singing, "Saul has struck down his thousands, and David his ten thousands" (18:7). Everyone was joyful and celebrating—everyone except Saul.

Verse 8 tells us that Saul was very angry because the people were honoring David above him, crediting David with ten times the victories that he'd had. I love way the English

Standard Version translates the next line: "Saul eyed David from that day on" (18:9). Saul stared daggers at David and lived in the detrimental land of jealousy.

Then, the day after the celebration, "a harmful spirit from God rushed upon Saul" (18:10),[1] and he raved around in the palace as David played his lyre. Saul took a spear and hurled it at David in order to pin him to the wall. It's tempting to write this off as the action of a madman, but I think Saul knew exactly what he was doing. A person doesn't just randomly decide to hurl a spear at someone, and certainly no one repeatedly tries to harm someone who has faithfully served him. This was a premeditated act to get rid of David. Verse 14 says, "David had success in all his undertakings, for the LORD was with him," and verse 15 tells us that Saul feared David because he saw his "great success."

Rather than turning to the Lord so he could make sense of his situation, Saul handled his fear in his own way—by doing everything he could think of to get rid of David. At first he tried to marry him to his daughter Merab. Now if we remember from chapter 17, part of the prize for defeating Goliath was getting to marry the king's daughter. But Saul now added the stipulation that to marry Merab, David must be valiant and fight for him (see 18:17). Saul thought that David would die in battle with the Philistines and that he wouldn't have to throw a spear at him anymore.

But David hesitated, humbly claiming that because he hadn't come from royal blood, it wouldn't be right for him to be the king's son-in-law. So Saul gave Merab to someone else. Then Saul got wind of the fact that his other daughter, Michal, loved David. Saul thought, "Let me give her to him, that she may be a snare for him and that the hand of the Philistines may be against him" (18:21). (I wonder what Saul knew about his daughter that made him think she'd be a snare for David!) So Saul invited David to be his son-in-law again, and this time he told his servants to encourage David to take the deal.

But once more, David hesitated. In addition to the argument of his weak family background, David added that he was a poor man who couldn't afford to pay the dowry for Michal. (Note David's continuous humility.) So Saul made David an offer he couldn't refuse: "The king desires no bride-price except a hundred foreskins of the Philistines" (18:25). Again, Saul thought he could get rid of David by sending him off to die in battle. Well, David went to battle, but he didn't die. Instead, he actually killed *two* hundred Philistines and brought their foreskins back.[2] So Saul gave David his daughter Michal. The chapter ends with these verses:

> When Saul saw and knew that the LORD was with David, and that Michal, Sauls's daughter, loved him, Saul was even more afraid of David. So Saul was David's enemy continually. Then the princes of the Philistines came out to battle, and as often as they came out David had more success than all the servants of Saul, so that his name was highly esteemed. (18:28–30)

While Saul ended up bitter and fearful, David ended up popular and revered. Saul and David made decisions that led them to their final positions.

Success is not so much an endpoint but a series of choices and actions that build upon one another. And as we'll see, success done God's way often looks quite different from that gained by the methods people often use.

The Real Definition of Success

David obtained success by serving well wherever God placed him. When he played the harp, he put in 110 percent. When he was Saul's armor bearer, he put in 110 percent. When he was a captain over one thousand men, he put in 110 percent. Always obedient to the authority placed over him, David put his whole heart into his service and trusted God for the results.

Saul's approach was very different. Position was very important to Saul, and he strived to appear successful, to be revered and to receive honor—whether he deserved it or not. Saul was constantly comparing himself to others, which is why he became so upset when the woman sang about David killing tens of thousands when he himself had only killed thousands. (Note that David wasn't trying to compete with Saul; he was focused on bringing God glory and honor—not aggrandizing himself.) Saul's self-serving attitude made him jealous and bitter when he should have instead been thankful for David's service and dedication.

David never tried to convince people that he was great; his actions spoke for his heart. When the women were singing and dancing about David's greatness, it wasn't because David had been out there campaigning for himself. David let God handle his public relations; in other words, he trusted God with his destiny, and God blessed him for his servant's heart. The people liked David and were pleased when Saul set David over the warriors not because David tried to manipulate their opinions of him but because he honestly and wisely did his job and let God work.

Saul, however, took his destiny into his own hands. He tried to control every situation in order to appear important and powerful. He didn't like all the attention David was getting, so he made him the head of a thousand men so that David would end up in dangerous battles and get killed. He offered his daughters to David in marriage as a plot to kill him. He tried to manipulate David by having his servants whisper things in David's ear. Saul was always trying to work situations to his advantage.

In First Samuel 13, as we noted earlier, Saul decided to offer the sacrifice instead of waiting for Samuel to arrive as the Lord had told him to. Then when God told Saul to destroy the Amalekites in chapter 15, Saul intentionally acted against God's instructions again. Saul was focused on protecting and advancing himself rather than on honoring the Lord, and his disobedience to the Lord ironically led him far from success.

Although Saul and David fought similar battles, they responded to those battles very differently. Whereas David put God first, others second and himself last, Saul was always thinking of himself first. So how did each of these guys' plans work out?

The largest difference in the fruit of these two men's lives was that David enjoyed closeness to the Lord and Saul did not. But there were several other results of Saul's and David's actions.

First, David was able to take praise and still remain humble, but Saul was captivated by others' praise and opinions. David had spent his life out in a field by himself caring for his dad's sheep. He was the youngest, so his brothers were always putting him down and teasing him. Outside his family, no one probably knew his name. But then he won the battle against Goliath, and suddenly the entire nation was celebrating him. It had to have been tough for someone so removed from society to be suddenly that visible and popular.

All that praise could really have gone to David's head. But David didn't come off the battlefield tooting his own horn, and he didn't make a big show of his victory. Instead, he happily transitioned to playing the harp in Saul's court. David didn't worry about promotion or demotion, about whether or not he was climbing the political ladder. He simply did what was required of him in every situation. The way David went after success allowed him to be free. Because David's identity was in the Lord, it didn't matter to him whether he was alone listening to the breeze or in a stadium full of people cheering his name. David was revered because he went after success the right way. His nation's people loved him. His fellow soldiers loved him. Even Saul loved him at first.

Saul, on the other hand, in his striving for recognition and praise, consistently lost respect. When he made the command in First Samuel 14 that none of his men should eat during the battle and then had to rescind it, he lost his men's respect. When Goliath threatened and mocked the Israelite army, Saul should have stepped up to fight him, trusting the Lord to bring the victory. But he didn't, because he was afraid. And then in chapter 18 Saul was raving mad within his palace and plagued with frustration and anxiety. These things certainly don't engender respect. Saul's insistence on following his own way slowly destroyed him.

Second, David trusted in God through the up-and-down circumstances of his life, and the Lord honored David's commitment to Him by staying with David every step of his way. Verses 12, 14 and 28 of First Samuel 18 tell us that the Lord was with David. David was able to be flexible, to accept what life threw at him, because he trusted that God was working in and through him—even when he couldn't see how. David's faith was rewarded with the best thing possible: more of God.

But Saul had no interest in leaving matters in God's hands! He sought to manipulate events for his own ends. Trying to control our destiny can lead not only to our ruin—it can lead to God actively opposing us. We're told in James 4:6 that God opposes the proud. Because of Saul's pride and disobedience, God departed from Saul (see 1 Sam. 18:12). So when Saul's plans didn't go as he expected, he didn't have the peace of the Lord to comfort him. Instead, he became anxious, angry and upset. He couldn't handle the pressure.

Third, because of his honest heart, David was able to build strong relationships. The people trusted him, the soldiers followed him, and even Saul's daughters liked him! David also gave Saul the benefit of the doubt even after Saul *threw a javelin at him*. Talk about a dedicated employee!

Saul, however, trusted no one. He didn't trust his own family to support him, and he didn't even trust God's priests. Saul's way to "success" certainly didn't foster good relationships.

In addition to all the other benefits, David had freedom, whereas Saul suffered from fear. Throughout First Samuel 18 it seems as if David can't lose and Saul can't win—and this is partially because of their attitudes: David trusted God for victory; Saul worried when he wasn't at the top of the chain.

The Search for Success

Why is it that David's method for success worked, and what can we learn from that method? The word "success" is mentioned four times in First Samuel 18 (see 18:5, 14, 15, 30). I'm no Greek or Hebrew scholar, but I think it's important to look at the original translations here. The Hebrew word *sakal* can be translated "to behave wisely," "to have a capacity for understanding" or "to prosper." These definitions help us understand true success. People who are going to be successful are prudent and wisely seek to understand God and His ways. They know what God likes and dislikes, and they align their behavior with the way God operates.

This is a very good description of David's success. Is it any wonder that in this same passage we're told three times that the Lord was with David? David knew who God was; and he sought to make his life match up with God's desires. David prospered because of his wisdom.

Sometimes in our society we get tripped up by a desire to appear wealthy and powerful, and we start striving for success the way Saul did. Rather than seeking the Lord's wisdom, we run on our own limited intelligence, and we miss out on being a *sakal* kind of person. We rob ourselves of real prosperity by failing to strive for real success. In Jeremiah 9:23–24, the Lord declares,

> Let not the wise man boast in his wisdom, let not the mighty man boast in his might, let not the rich man boast in his riches, but let him who boasts boast in this, that he understands and

knows me, that I am the LORD, who practices steadfast love, justice, and righteousness in the earth. For in these things I delight.

In other words, don't boast in intelligence or might or money, because none of those are the source of success. God tells us here what the real source of success is. When the Lord says that we should boast about understanding Him, He uses that same term *sakal*. If we want true success, we have to seek to know our kind, loving, powerful and upright God.

Staying on the Path

A man named Richard Stearns accepted the Lord at age twenty-three, when he was in college working on his master's degree. He was serious about his commitment to God, and he developed the life mantra to always love, serve and obey the Lord. He got out of college, married and went to work for Parker Brothers, where he received promotion after promotion until he became the president of the company. All along the way, he shared Christ with others and tried to honor the Lord in everything he did. Then Parker Brothers sold the company, and Richard lost his job.

A couple years later Richard started working for Lenox, a fine-china company. Again he steadily worked his way up the corporate ladder until 1995, when he became president and CEO of the entire company. He lived in a ten-bedroom home on five acres of land just outside Philadelphia, Pennsylvania. He drove a Jaguar and traveled extensively—always flying first-class and staying in the best hotels. He was a believer and was highly respected in the community.

Then in 1998, just three years after becoming president of Lenox, he received a call from a recruiter asking if he would consider being the president of World Vision. (World Vision is a Christian humanitarian organization working to care for abandoned, exploited and otherwise underprivileged and at-risk children.) Now what I didn't mention was that Richard had grown up in poverty. When he was a boy, his parents got a divorce and lost their house; they lived from paycheck to paycheck. Richard wasn't keen on giving up the position at Lenox that he had worked so hard to obtain, so he said no to World Vision several times. He didn't know anything about global poverty or relief and development or fundraising. *Why are they asking me?* he wondered.

One day the recruiter from World Vision called and asked, "Are you willing to be open to God's will for your life?" Richard answered, "Yes, but . . ." He had a long list of reasons why taking the position with World Vision would be a huge mistake: he didn't know how to do the job, he'd worked over twenty years to get to the top of Lenox, he'd have to uproot his family and take a 75 percent pay cut.

Then Richard and his wife went to a church service at which the speaker spoke of children all around the world who are dying of hunger, who are suffering and who need the gospel. Richard and his wife came home and broke down crying, because they recognized that God was calling them. Richard said, "God broke me, and I knew that I could no longer run from him."[3]

God broke Richard away from the route of success that Saul had taken. Now Richard didn't seek success out of selfish greed and pride in the way Saul had done; Richard was a believer who strove to love, serve and obey the Lord with his whole life. But financial stability, pride in his work and a prestigious title distracted him from the true success that comes from fully trusting the Lord.

Richard is a first-class guy. His story makes me stop and say, "Wow!" because if he could be pushed off track, so could any of us. So I ask: Could this be happening to us? How are we searching after success?

There's a great old song that says, "Whatever it takes for my will to break, that's what I'll be willing to do."[4] What needs to be broken in our lives? We need to ask the Lord to search our hearts and to show us where we need to make changes so we can follow His plan for success. I pray that we will hold our security, our plans and our ideas of success with an open hand so that the Lord can mold us into His image. I'm not saying that this is easy, but it is good. It's the way David lived, and he was blessed. And it's the way Richard learned to live. We're happiest and most fruitful when we're living for the Lord. *That* is real success.

Let's Pray:

Lord God, thank You for shifting our ideas on what it means to be successful. Teach us to trust You as You hold our lives in Your hand. Hold us, and mold us into Your likeness. In Jesus' name, amen.

CHAPTER SIX

DAVID AND JONATHAN:
THE NEED FOR REAL FRIENDSHIP

1 Samuel 20

Pastor Marty Berglund

Jonathan said to David, "Go in peace, for we have sworn both of us in the name of the LORD, saying, 'The LORD shall be between me and you, and between my offspring and your offspring, forever.'"
1 Samuel 20:42

God never meant for us to function in an isolated bubble. He created us for community, and He expects us, like David did, to make friendships with other believers who will challenge and encourage us. Of course, that involves some sacrifice on our part; friendships require effort and commitment. David invested in the life of Saul's son, Jonathan, and because of that, he was blessed with a genuine friend.

In case the Bible's commands aren't enough to convince us of the importance of relationship, I want to highlight the story of David and Jonathan—an example of true, dedicated friendship. In First Samuel 20 Scripture goes into detail about David and Jonathan not just to move the plot along but to show us the foundations and benefits of real camaraderie.

David and Jonathan: Dos Amigos

David and Jonathan were not likely friends. David grew up on a farm taking care of animals, whereas Jonathan was raised in a palace. But this kid from the wrong side of the tracks and this rich kid got to be friends because of David's musical talent. Saul brought David into his home—which is also where Jonathan lived—to play the harp for him. While Scripture doesn't go into a lot of detail, David and Jonathan probably hung out together when David wasn't working. Then David slew Goliath, and he became a champion, just as Jonathan had become when he had attacked and killed twenty Philistines all by himself. David and Jonathan were tough guys, and despite their disparate upbringings, they formed a close, close friendship.

Fast forward a few years, and we have Saul, Jonathan's dad, going crazy and hurling spears at David. David was reasonably concerned about the event and went to Jonathan, his close confidante, to ask his opinion on the whole ordeal. I'm a preacher and not a Hollywood man, but please bear with me as I present a short screenplay of the story of David and Jonathan:

David: Yo, Jonathan. What's going on here? Did I do something wrong? Why is your dad trying to kill me?

Jonathan: Dad doesn't do anything without telling me first. There's no way he wants you dead.

David: I don't know, man. Saul knows that we're friends, so he probably wouldn't want to tell you if he's plotting to kill me, because he knows it would upset you. I'm telling you—he's trying to get rid of me.

Jonathan: Whatever you ask me to do, I'll do.

David: Tomorrow is the New Moon Festival. I'm supposed
            to be at the feast at Saul's table, but instead I'm going
            to hide in a field. If your dad misses me, tell him
            that I asked you for permission to go to Bethlehem
            to make a yearly sacrifice for my family. If Saul says,
            "Good," then I'm probably in the clear. But if he
            gets upset, then we'll know he plans to hurt me.
            Please be kind and help me, and remember that we
            made a covenant before the Lord to support one
            another. That said, if I've done something wrong,
            then don't bother waiting to let your father finish
            me off. Just kill me now yourself.

Jonathan: Absolutely not! Don't you know that if Dad had
            told me he planned to harm you, I'd have told you
            immediately?

David: All right. Then how will I know if Saul gets angry
            when I'm not at the feast?

Jonathan: With God, the Lord of Israel, as my witness, I
            promise you that I will let you know Saul's intentions
            once I've felt him out on the matter, which will
            either happen tomorrow or the next day. I honestly
            don't think he'd harm you, but if I'm wrong, may
            God Himself harm me all the more if I don't tell
            you so you can safely escape. May God be with you
            as He has been with Saul! If I'm still alive when
            you return someday, show me the steadfast love of
            the Lord and keep me from death. When the Lord
            wipes out all your enemies, please remember me
            and my descendants and show us kindness. Now
            tomorrow is the new moon, and you will be missed
            because your seat will be empty. Two days from now

go down to the same field where you hid before and stay close to the stone heap. I will shoot three arrows to the side of it and tell the boy with me to go collect them. If I say to him, "Look, the arrows are back this way," then come out of hiding for as surely the Lord lives, there is no danger. But if I say, "Look, the arrows are out further," then go, for the Lord has sent we away. And as for what we talked about earlier, remember that the Lord is between you and me forever.

Narrator: David hid himself in the field. When the new moon came, Saul sat down at his table to eat with the rest of his court. David's place was empty, but Saul thought that something must have made David unclean and therefore unable to attend the dinner, so he didn't worry about David's absence. But the next day, when David still didn't show up to eat, Saul asked Jonathan, "Why isn't David here?" Jonathan replied, "David asked me if he could go to Bethlehem to make a sacrifice with his family and to see his brothers." Saul became very angry with Jonathan and said, "You son of a perverse and rebellious woman! Don't you know that it's shameful for you to give your loyalties to David? As long as David lives, our kingdom will never rightly be established. So bring him to me; he must die!" Jonathan asked what David had done that he should die, and Saul responded by hurling his spear at him. When Jonathan realized that his father did indeed intend to kill David, he rose from the table in anger and refused to eat anything for an entire day. He was grieved for David that he should be treated so unjustly. The next day, Jonathan went out into the field as he had promised David. He shot three arrows out into the field. When the boy went to retrieve them, Jonathan called.

Jonathan: Look, the arrow is out past where you are. Hurry, be quick, and do not stay.

Narrator: The boy gathered up the arrows and returned to his master, and Jonathan told him to carry them back to the city. As soon as the boy left, David came out of hiding and fell on his face on the ground, bowing before Jonathan three times. The two men kissed one another and wept with one another.

Jonathan: Go in peace, because we have both sworn in the name of the Lord, "The Lord shall be between us and between your offspring and my offspring forever."

Narrator: So David rose and fled, and Jonathan returned to the city.

End scene.

The Value of Open Communication

David and Jonathan's bond lays the groundwork for us to understand true friendship. One of the key components of the relationship between these two young men was open communication. Look how the dialogue starts in First Samuel 20:1: "Then David fled from Naioth in Ramah and came and said before Jonathan, 'What have I done? What is my guilt? And what is my sin before your father, that he seeks my life?'" David started off with some serious questions; he didn't just come up to Jonathan and say, "Hey, what's up? How are you doing?" No, David was conflicted and dealing with something serious—namely that Saul, his king and employer, was trying to kill him—so he didn't beat around the bush with superficial dialogue. Jonathan reacted well to this immediate launch into serious conversation, so we have every reason to believe that the two men had shared their hearts with one another in the past and that they had a close enough relationship that they were comfortable being real with one another right from the get-go.

Unfortunately, many of us have friendships that never move past small talk to what's bothering us, to what's really on our minds and hearts. When we're not open and honest, we settle into superficial relationships that won't help us grow. We put on a social show that drains us instead of investing in someone who will be able to encourage and strengthen us.

First John 1:7 tells us, "But if we walk in the light, as he is in the light, we have fellowship with one another, and the blood of Jesus his Son cleanses us from all sin." What is walking in the light? It's being seen; it's being transparent in our actions; it's being open. Having fellowship with God is being honest with Him about our sin and opening our life to Him so He can work in and through us. Similarly, it's vital for us to be open in our relationships with other people. Sometimes God teaches, encourages, and helps us not through a direct word from heaven but rather through our Christian brothers and sisters. If we want God's care and direction, we should start by being open in our relationships.

Most of us have grown up in a society that ascribes value primarily to individual experience and strength, and so many of us have never learned how to live well in community. We don't learn the importance of being vulnerable and of sacrificing our time and energy for the sake of building others up. The New Testament tells us to care for one another, teach one another, admonish one another, bear one another's burdens, etc. That means that we have an active role to play, not just as the one helping but as the one being helped. Relationships are two-way streets.

It's clear from First Samuel 20 that God uses friends to strengthen us. God used Jonathan to help David become all that David needed to be, and Jonathan became what he needed to be because God used David in his life. We too need friends who will build us up and challenge us biblically.

The Importance of Relationship

"You know, Marty, I just don't have many friends," an acquaintance of mine from out West admitted to me over the phone. "I work all the time. I'm always busy taking care of clients and hiring and firing employees. And when I'm not tied up at the office, I'm running back and forth to the kids' soccer games and football practice. I'm all over the place." We can probably identify with some piece of Rob's story. It's the norm in America to work long hours and to place high value on busy schedules.

It's good and biblical to be dedicated to our work, but it becomes a problem when it starts interfering with our relationships. In a land that values self above all else, we need to learn the power of true friendship—and that starts with, once again, examining our hearts. Rob continued, "I'll be honest with you. I go to church, but that's really all I do—I just go. There aren't many people my age there, and I don't have any friends in the church. In fact, none of my close friends are Christians, and I'm really starting to feel that lack."

If we attend a church but don't have any friends there, then we've missed the whole point of church. A lot of Christians think of church as an event—as something they either want to do or feel like they should do on a Sunday. But if we read the New Testament, we see that God designed church as a way for believers to build community. "Doing church" should mean getting involved in the lives of the other people who are "doing church." We should get into small groups and get to know the people around us. We shouldn't wait for other people to approach and welcome us; we should take the step to reach out to them. Church is supposed to be a place where a group of people—Christ's body—meets with God. And listen—no one in the church is perfect. But when we invest in the lives of our Christian brothers and sisters, they'll invest in ours, and we'll learn how to grow together. We need to step out on faith, trust God and build some real friendships.

God created human beings for relationship. One of our greatest needs—aside from being in relationship with God Himself—is to be in community and fellowship with other people. The Ten Commandments of the Old Testament are all about relationships, how to properly behave in community with the Lord and with His people, and the New Testament too is filled with commands to care for and encourage one another. In fact, Jesus summed up the greatest commandments as loving God and loving others as we love ourselves (see Matt. 22:37–39). But even within the church, we sometimes take the gift of friendship too lightly—as if it's optional to invest in others' lives.

My friend Rob had a real need, so I challenged him, "Who in your life might you might be able to connect with?" Rob shared that he had been hurt by being vulnerable in the past—an unfortunately all-too-common predicament. But we have to step out and trust God. We have to surrender some of our pride as well as our insecurity and reach out to someone. We need to share our lives and our stories—where we're going, where we're not going, what God is teaching us and what we're struggling to understand. It requires some vulnerability, but it's important.

I remember when I was a little boy and my dad's best friend Floyd Gustav Johnson would come over to visit. Since his friend's middle name was Gustav, Dad called him Goose. Goose and Dad were both blue-collar factory workers, and they enjoyed going hunting and fishing together as well as chatting for hours on end. I remember the two of them spending entire evenings sitting in our living room, eating ice cream or whatever was on hand, and discussing their lives. When I was eight or ten years old, I would sit and listen to them. I think that was my introduction to real friendship.

My Dad died when I was thirty, and his funeral service was packed with friends and people whose lives he had touched. I remember my older brother crying and saying, "Man, I just hope some day I have friends like Dad had friends." One of the most valuable things we can do in this life is to invest in the lives of others. To use a popular phrase in the church these days, we need to "do life" with other believers—welcoming them into our world and being willing to go through life's messes together.

Facing Life's What-ifs Together

I went to seminary in Dallas, Texas and the head of the Christian Counseling Center down there was a prominent and leading psychologist with about fifty other trained counselors on his staff. This ministry had a huge impact on the community. One day the psychologist came to speak at my seminary, and he said, "Gentlemen, if the church really functioned as God intended and people were really as close to one another as the New Testament indicates they're supposed to be, I'd be out of business. I'd say that all that 80 to 90 percent of my clients need is a friend."

Again, he is a psychologist. He makes a living addressing people's mental and emotional illnesses, and he calls himself—his words—"a paid friend." People don't realize how badly they need someone to help them process the "what-ifs" of life. Look at verses 6 and 7, and pay close attention to how many times David uses the word "if": "If your father misses me at all, tell him, 'David earnestly asked my permission to hurry to Bethlehem, his hometown, because an annual sacrifice is being made there for his whole clan.' If he says, 'Very well,' then your servant is safe. But if he loses his temper, you can be sure that he is determined to harm me." David wasn't certain what his future held, so he got together with Jonathan, and they worked through the what-ifs together.

One of the keys to deep friendship is processing the what-ifs of life with another person. Introverted or extroverted, academically brilliant or incompetent—none of us are capable of functioning at our highest potential without others' influence. We all have what-ifs about our careers, our health, our marriages, and some of us may struggle with things like depression or burnout or anger—just because we haven't allowed anyone in to help us. We were never meant to figure out life on our own. We need to enlist others to help us process our what-ifs.

I've had several church friends who have helped me process big decisions and little concerns. They're not necessarily elders or staff; they're just people who have devoted the time and energy necessary to care for others. I enjoy doing things with them, but in the end, it's not about the activity we share but about having time to chat and work through life with them. I think I finally understand the relationship my dad and Goose had as they enjoyed just being together and talking through things.

We have a tendency to get upset and bitter that good friends don't just fallen into our lap, but I want reaffirm that friendships take effort. That said, the best way to make friends isn't to look for them; rather, we find friends by working to care for and serve other people. Let me give an example.

My daughter and her husband are leaders in Young Life (an organization that introduces Christ to adolescents) in northeastern Pennsylvania. One kid who has been in their group for a couple years now is a bit of an odd duck. There are football players and cheerleaders and all sorts of people in their group, but this kid stands out because he's socially awkward and an unusual guy all around. A while back his mom came to my daughter and told her, "Thank you so much for what you've done for my son. He's a changed person." His mom said that the way the other kids in the group had loved him, accepted him, talked with him and simply befriended him had totally changed her son's life perspective. She explained that he had a new joy and zest for life.

My daughter told me that she's so glad this boy is in their group, because reaching out to him has shown the other kids the importance of being friends to others. It's shown them how enriching a simple friendly gesture can be and the impact it can make. I think my daughter is right on point. We have to be friends to make friends. Sometimes we have to engage in others' what-ifs before they will feel comfortable enough to invest in ours.

Each of us has to be intentional about getting into real relationship. It's necessary for us to ask (and be willing to answer) the hard questions in order to find out the truth of what's going on in a person's life. Working toward deep friendship requires us to dig deeper than "How are you?" "Fine. How are you?" Relationships can get hard and messy, but it's important for us to reject the impulse to have all the answers. With our friends we need to search Scripture together, wait on the Lord together and trust the Lord for outcomes together. Then we'll be able to praise God for His answers to our what-ifs together.

Commit Friendships to the Lord

Look at the last verse of First Samuel 20: "Jonathan said to David, 'Go in peace, because we have sworn both of us in the name of the LORD, saying, 'The LORD shall be between me and you, and between my offspring and your offspring, forever.'" Jonathan thought that maybe if David did end up rising to power and becoming king (as Saul had hinted at earlier), David might kill Jonathan and his offspring. As far as Jonathan knew, the opposite could be true too—that he might become king and have reason to kill all David's descendants. That's what kings did back then to protect their reign. But David and Jonathan made a peace treaty, swearing to each other and before the Lord that if either of them ended up in power, each of them would do his best to take care of the other's family.

This type of pact probably isn't necessary in today's friendships. It certainly isn't in any of mine. But the applicable piece of this verse is that David and Jonathan were both, in a sense, surrendering. To be a true friend to someone, some surrender has to take place. We have to devote time and energy to the relationship. We have to trust that person with information about us, and we have to open our heart to him or her. And oftentimes when we do that, we get hurt. Risk is involved, but it's necessary to take that risk in order to enjoy the fulfillment of true friendship. In the same way that marriage covenants are designed as declarations of trust and commitment from the man and woman involved, David and Jonathan drew up a covenant saying that they were in their friendship for the long haul and that they were trusting each other and the Lord with the results. Why shouldn't we be committed to our friends in the same way?

So what the glue is that holds true friendships together? It's God. When we honor the Lord, He gives us friends to remind us of His truths and to help encourage and direct us. He wants us to understand the value of and experience the power of devoted friends.

Stop thinking that friendship is optional, because that's not what Scripture teaches. We all need to search for a few believers whose lives we can truly invest in. We need to practice being transparent and honest. If we don't trust others and don't have friends to help us process life's what-ifs, we emotionally handicap ourselves.

I pray that we decide to trust God and ask Him to help each of us be better friends. I pray that we say, "Okay, Lord, I want a friend, and I want to be a friend. Show me how." Then I pray that we will trust God—knowing that He'll use our friends in the faith to speak to us and minister to us. May the Lord bless us to enjoy close, heartfelt friendships like that of David and Jonathan!

Let's pray:

Lord, in Your name, we thank You for the opportunity to have authentic friendships. Guide us to those who will serve us well and whom we can also serve with our whole hearts. Amen.

CHAPTER SEVEN

DAVID IN DESPERATION:
MAINTAINING FAITH WHEN EVERYTHING'S GOING WRONG

1 Samuel 19, 21

Pastor Glenn Kantner

*I cry to you, O LORD; I say, "You are my refuge, my portion in the
land of the living." Attend to my cry, for I am brought very low!
Deliver me from my persecutors, for they are too strong for me!
Psalm 142:5–6*

Our perspectives can get clouded from time to time. We put
hope in our abilities, finances, spouses or jobs, and when
circumstances take a turn for the worse, our hope drops. Our
hearts at times turn away from following the Lord's instructions.
But if we train ourselves to continually trust God more and
more, then when we get into a truly desperate situation, we will
find that instead of collapsing, our hope will hold firm and even
be strengthened.

Obviously, desperation without faith in God doesn't
bring about hope. Meditating on the fact that we're in a dark pit
won't get us out of our mess. But desperation can be a tool that
drives us to focus on the right things.

David's Journey to Desperation

David's life started out pretty well. He spent his days tending sheep in the field and playing music. Then he got a big break and ended up being a national war hero and living in the king's palace. The people loved him, and he had a wife who cared about him and a best friend who vowed to watch out for him. Up until First Samuel 19, I think it's fair to say that David was blessed in the way we typically consider "blessing"—which is to say that he was popular, financially stable and in a position of power. But by chapter 21 everything in David's life was really falling apart. One thing after another went wrong, until he ended up in a cave by himself with nowhere left to go and no one to turn to. He was desperate and despairing. So he started asking why questions: *Why did You let me get here, God? Why are You doing this to me?*

Let's walk though his journey. In the first verse of First Samuel 19, Saul told his son Jonathan and all his attendants to kill David if they saw him. But because Jonathan cared for David, he went to Saul to tell him that David hadn't done anything wrong, and he talked his dad out of his decision to get rid of David. Then Jonathan brought David back to the palace, where David reassumed his lyre-playing responsibilities. But before long, that evil spirit we talked about before came on Saul again, and Saul chucked a javelin at David a third time.

David escaped and went home, but when he got there, his wife Michal warned him, "If you do not escape with your life tonight, tomorrow you will be killed" (19:11). Michal helped David escape through a window, and David went to live with Samuel. Saul caught wind of this news and sent men to kill David.

Now Samuel ran a small private school that taught men how to become prophets. When Saul's men reached Samuel's place, the Spirit of God fell upon them, and despite the fact that they weren't men of God, they started prophesying and were unable to kill David. Saul sent a second group, and the same thing happened. So he sent a third group, and guess what? They all started prophesying too. Saul finally decided that if he wanted the job done right, he would have to do it himself, so he set off to take care of David. But when he reached Naoith at Ramah, the Spirit came upon him as well, and he lay on the ground prophesying (see 19:18–24). Crazy!

I don't know why David didn't stay with Samuel. Maybe he thought the prophesying couldn't last forever. At any rate, he got scared, and without consulting God, he left Samuel and ran to talk to Jonathan. That's the story we looked at when David chose not to attend Saul's big banquet. David and Jonathan said their sorrowful goodbye, and David took off once again—still without asking God what he should do (see 1 Sam. 20).

From there David went to Nob to visit the priest Ahimelech. He was hungry, so he asked for some bread and conjured up a story about being on a mission for the king. The only bread available was what the priests called the showbread.[1] David fibbed his way into getting some food and then asked if Ahimelech had a weapon he could take—lying again and saying that he hadn't brought a sword with him because his mission required haste. "The priest said, 'The sword of Goliath the Philistine, whom you struck down in the Valley of Elah, behold, it is here wrapped in a cloth behind the ephod. If you will take that, take it, for there is none but that here.' And David said, 'There is none like that; give it to me'" (21:9).

David took Goliath's sword and—once more without consulting the Lord—fled to Achish, the king of Gath. I think David must have asked himself, *Where is the last place on earth Saul would show up?* He decided his best bet would be to go deep into enemy territory, so he paid the Philistines a visit. David probably hoped he wouldn't be recognized, but his enemies immediately identified him as the one about whom the people sang, "David has killed his tens of thousands" (see 21:10). This seems like it should have been a "duh moment" for David. Gath was Goliath's hometown. David had killed the Philistines' hero and then later killed two hundred Philistines and circumcised them to pay the bride price for Michal. Of course those guys knew who he was, and they didn't like him one bit.

Achish's servants grabbed David and took him to the king. David knew the Philistines would tear him apart limb by limb for what he had done to their people, and he was scared. Because he was desperate, David made an odd move. He decided to pretend he was insane, so he made marks on the doors of the gate and let spit drip down his beard. In that day people thought mental disabilities were punishments for offending a god, so men wouldn't go near a person who appeared to be insane. When the men brought David into Achish's court, Achish was frustrated: "Behold, you see the man is mad. Why then have you brought him to me? Do I lack madmen, that you have brought this fellow to behave as a madman in my presence? Shall this fellow come into my house?" (21:14–15). David was set free, and he took off again, this time escaping to the cave of Adullam (see 22:1).

Notice that along David's journey, his efforts kept getting him deeper and deeper in trouble. Because he didn't consult God along the way, he put himself and his friends in danger. Jonathan almost got killed when Saul threw a spear at him. Michal was punished for helping David escape. And remember the priest who gave David the bread? Saul found out about the exchange and had all Nob's priests (eighty-five in total) and their families killed. Now it's true that Saul is the one who perpetrated these horrible crimes out of anger and jealousy, but David's scheming—and notably his lack of consulting God—regrettably helped lead to the loss of many innocent lives.

After several wrong turns, David hit rock bottom and found himself sitting in a cave and wondering what to do next. (Read Psalm 142 if you want a glimpse of what was running through his mind.) David ended up alone, feeling depressed and lost. Talk about a contrast from the confident, popular David of the earlier chapters! But ending up in the cave was a good thing for David, because it made him reach the end of himself. It made him realize he needed to stop trying to control his situation and give it to God.

Desperate Enough to Give It All to God

What was true for David is true for us. Our first, human reaction to problems is typically to try to solve things on our own. We try to control our situations until we finally realize that there are some things we can't work out. We've probably been in a "cave" before, feeling as if the walls were closing in on us and wondering if we'd ever see the light again.

I've been talking for the past couple years with a woman in my church who has been in a cave. Due to an injury at her job, she's disabled, and for whatever reason she's slipped through all the cracks of our social system, so she's not getting disability or worker's compensation. She has no income, and she's trying to support her family by herself. Whenever I used to talk to her, it was always the same story: "My electric/heating/water bill is due next week. If I don't somehow find three hundred dollars to pay it, they'll shut the electricity/heat/water off, and then how will the kids and I make it?!" Through years of struggling, this lady learned how to get what she needed, yet it still seemed as if she was in one crisis or another.

I spoke to her after Pastor Berglund had preached one day about David and Goliath and about how to beat the giants in our lives, and this woman sounded like an entirely different person. She said, "Tuesday they're going to turn my water off unless I can pay the bill." Then she added, "But you know what? It's the Lord's battle." She's still being proactive about her situation, but now she's doing things not out of desperation but in faith. Now she's saying, "If the Lord provides through the government, then great, but if He doesn't, then He must know we don't need water, and that's okay. He's the one fighting this battle now." There's a new peace in her heart. When we trust God like that, God works on our behalf.

Desperate Enough to Recognize the Lord's Supernatural Presence

When our desperation drives us to the point at which we recognize the supernatural presence of the Lord, we can have hope in any circumstance. David's problem was that he was looking only at the difficulty. He allowed his fear to get the upper hand, and he ran. Why didn't David stay with Samuel? It was like he expected God's favor and defense to run out. Then when Ahimelech gave him the holy bread—a symbol of the Lord's presence—one would think he would have been reminded that God was with him, but David wasn't. And when David was given Goliath's sword, it seems as if he would have remembered that God had been with him when he had faced the giant and had won the battle for him, but David was focused on his own concerns rather than on the Lord's faithfulness. David couldn't stop thinking about what Saul might do to him long enough to be able to recognize God's protection. So God had to keep taking things away from David—person by person—until all David had was God and the cave.

In the cave David came to his senses. Psalm 142, written during David's stay in Adullam, reads, "I cry to you, O Lord; I say, 'You are my refuge, my portion in the land of the living'" (Ps. 142:5). David finally realized that God was his only refuge. He took his eyes off his problem long enough to put his eyes on the Lord—his true protection and hope.

My wife and I are friends with a couple—Bob and Ruth—who have faced some days as equally dark as David's. Bob had blood clots throughout his body, and the doctors couldn't determine a cause. Bob ended up having two open-heart surgeries within a month of each other, and the surgeons pulled out blood clots as large as a man's fist. Science tells us that Bob shouldn't have made it through—but he did. At the same time Ruth was battling breast cancer. She couldn't undergo the normal cancer treatments because of other medical issues she had, so she had to pursue alternative procedures. It was a hard time for both of them—trying to support one another while each of them was facing daunting news from their own doctors.

But God brought healing to Bob and Ruth. Bob is back at work and now able to walk around the block. Ruth's tumor has been shrinking. Or I should say it *had* been shrinking. We recently received an e-mail from Ruth saying that the shrinkage had leveled off. She writes, "Just when I think that the battle is under control, God reminds me of David's words to Goliath: 'The battle is not yours; but the Lord's.' So my heart needs prayers for focusing on the Leader of this battle instead of looking at my enemy, this giant of cancer."

Think about where Ruth is coming from. She's in the midst of a serious battle, and she and her husband had just come out of some desperate circumstances; they were both close to death's door many times. Ruth's story is incredible; she learned to lean on God, and she says His Word became the food that kept her going. But Ruth admits that when her situation got better, she reverted to placing her hope in her circumstances rather than in the Lord. As a result, when the tumor stopped shrinking, her hope started dropping. She realized what had happened, so she asked for prayer that she might place her hope back in the eternal God who has the supernatural power to do whatever needs to be done.

When we get desperate—when all life's distractions are peeled away and we're confronted with the severity of reality— we remember how essential it is to hope in the Lord and to remember that He is with us. But when things start going well, we can tend to switch our faith off, so to speak. We often fail to actively seek God, because we don't feel like we need Him as much as we did before. But if we really stop to think about it, we should be desperate all the time, living in a sinful world as we do. We deeply need God *all the time*, and we shouldn't have to end up in a dark, lonely cave before we turn our focus on Him. We must learn to be desperate enough all the time to recognize the supernatural presence and power of God in our daily life.

Desperate Enough to Accept God's Purpose and Provision

Desperation can also bring us to the point of being willing to accept God's purpose and provision for our lives. That's what happened to David in the cave. Look at another psalm he wrote when he was there:

> Be merciful to me, O God, be merciful to me,
>   for in you my soul takes refuge;
> in the shadow of your wings I will take refuge,
>   till the storms of destruction pass by.
> I cry out to God Most High,
>   to God who fulfills his purpose for me. (Ps. 57:1–2)

I'm sure it took some serious reflection and repentance for David to be able to write these verses. God's promises had not played out the way David had probably expected. After all, God had promised to make David king; He had *anointed* him king. But even though David hadn't yet entered his kingship, he submitted to God's purpose for him. Even though David was questioning why he had to go through so many dark days, he said, "God fulfills His purpose for me." He accepted his circumstances as being from God, no matter how difficult they appeared, and he trusted God to accomplish His plans through them. David was content for God's purposes, rather than his own, to be fulfilled.

We could summarize what happened to David as a result of his desperation in one word: brokenness. David went through a long, hard process to be rid of himself and his own ways—to recognize the presence of God. He ended up in a cave, broken before the Lord and recognizing that God's purposes were best for him.

Consider an acorn. An acorn has life inside of it, but it will never grow to become an oak tree unless its hard shell is broken, allowing a little green shoot to come out of it and take hold of the earth. As believers, we have the life of God within us. But that life of God isn't going to grow, isn't going to be visible to anybody else, unless we're broken. What has to break? Our old way of thinking, our old nature. Our own will has to be broken for the life of God to grow and develop. And the best way to crack the hard shell is to become desperate.

When my wife had an emergency appendectomy, I remember sitting alone outside the operating room, waiting and waiting. Her appendix had burst two days prior to the surgery, unbeknownst to any of us. I sat there at two o'clock in the morning, in the eerily quiet, dark prep room as the doctors prepared to cut into my wife. I sat there in silence, praying that everything would go smoothly and that my wife would be in the recovery room soon. An appendectomy is a pretty ordinary procedure, but I still found myself wondering, *What if something goes wrong?* So I began to do what David did. I told God, *Lord, it's Your plan. You know that I've come to the end of what I can do. I want my wife to live and to live well, but if losing her is part of Your plan, I still trust You and know that Your plan is best.*

That may sound like an odd prayer from a husband for his wife, but I promise I wasn't being harsh or unloving. Let me explain. I've been in similar places many times before. When I was twenty-three—right before I got married—I randomly started blacking out, and I lost feeling in my right arm. I didn't know if I'd be able to raise or support a family. None of the doctors could find anything wrong with me, so I recognized that I had come to the end of myself; I couldn't do anything to fix the situation. It was the first time I remember being truly broken before God. I had to recognize the presence of the supernatural God in my life and say, "Okay, God. It's Your plan, and I submit to it."

Over and over again throughout my life, I've run into situations like that—with health, with jobs that went sour, with challenging relationships. Every time God has pounded the lesson home: "You have to be broken to fully know Me." I'm not going to lie and say that I like the breaking process. But over the years I've learned to trust, because I always love the end result. I'm thankful for the hope, joy and peace that come from knowing that God is working out His purposes in me.

It's good to get so desperate that we lose our own way and latch onto God. It's good to be broken. We don't want to miss out on the blessing waiting on the other side of our difficulty by wallowing in pain in the dark. Instead, we need to trust God's supernatural power to bring new life out of our brokenness. When we're in a dark cave, we need to do what David did. Having a heart after God involves coming to the end of what we can do and giving our struggles to God in desperation. Then He'll give us new hope.

Let's pray:

Dear Lord, we desperately seek Your face. We seek Your guidance in all things. Thank You for meeting us in our desperation and for shining Your warm light in the dark and cold places of our lives. In Jesus' name, amen.

CHAPTER EIGHT

DAVID GETS OUT OF THE CAVE: UNEARTHING GOD'S PLAN FOR US

1 Samuel 23:1–18

Pastor Marty Berglund

Arise, go down to Keilah, for I will give the Philistines into your hand.
1 Samuel 23:4

There are basically only two ways of looking at life. The first is the natural way, and it involves trying to squeeze as much out of life as possible before we die. This method revolves around self-satisfaction and striving to gain recognition, cash, power and respect. The second, and opposing, life view is presented in the Bible. It states that each of us is created by God and that God has a specific purpose for every person. If what it says is true, then the best thing we can do is get in on God's plan for us. When we approach life this way, we don't need to fear death, because death is just another step in God's process—another piece of the journey God has for us. I can say from experience that God's plan is always greater than we can ever imagine.

God has a specific process for each one of us, and He's waiting for us to surrender our false concepts of control so He can show us real fullness. When we ask God to direct us, He leads us into His best. He restores us from our brokenness and gets us (and keeps us!) on the right track, close to His heart. But before we can go anywhere, we need to identify where we are now.

Compassion for Others Gets Us Out of Our Caves

David didn't stay in his cave for too long, because in his heart he still wanted the Lord's best for his life. Even though he had lost track of his purpose in several moments of fear, he eventually came to his senses and returned to the Lord. We too need to keep our hearts in a place of waiting on God.

After David had spent some time in Adullam, chillin' with a bunch of other discontented people who had heard about his misfortune and joined him in the cave (see 1 Sam. 22), a messenger came to report to David that some Philistines had attacked Keilah and were looting the threshing floors. That might not sound like an awful offense to us, but we need to consider what it was like to be part of a Hebrew family that owned a small farm. The father plowed the fields with his oxen, the mother and children sowed seeds and spread fertilizer, and they all simply prayed for the right amount of rain. A few months after the planting, they worked to harvest whatever hadn't been destroyed by disease or insects or animals. These families had a lot invested in the crop that the fields yielded, and they would need that food to survive the winter. So when these families from Keilah took their prized harvest to the threshing floor, and some Philistine fools came in and stole it all, it was a big deal.

David knew that the looting would have a tragic impact, and his heart went out to the victims in Keilah. David was touched by his fellow peoples' need, which lifted him out of his self-protective, self-absorbed mode. First Samuel 23:2 tells us, "Therefore David inquired of the LORD , 'Shall I go and attack these Philistines?'" and God told him to go. Note that David's immediate reaction was to go to God to ask Him what to do. The David of the Bible—the David after God's heart—had snapped back. Instead of worrying about what might happen to him, David once again submitted himself to the Lord's plans and asked God to show him what to do.

What we learn from this is that one of the best ways to get out of a cave is to be agitated by someone else's need—to open our self-protective shell enough to be touched by someone else who is greatly struggling. It may not make much sense to us to compound our problems by adding someone else's to them, but that's not actually what caring for others does. Instead, having our heart broken by others' problems gives us a broader perspective as well as a fresh sense of purpose to get out of our cave.

We've all seen television commercials from organizations like World Vision asking us to support starving children and struggling rural villages. Those ads aren't shown to make us feel guilty for having food or electricity or clean water. They're there to help get us out of our caves. Christ gave us the edict to "go therefore and make disciples of all nations, baptizing them in the name of the Father and of the Son and of the Holy Spirit, teaching them to observe all that I have commanded you" (Matt. 28:19–20) in order to spur us on to care for people across the globe. We can't say that helping someone isn't our responsibility, because Christ told us to share His light with the whole world— and that involves caring for the broken in Asia as well as for the hurting souls in our hometown. We need to think beyond ourselves as to how we can further the kingdom of God.

There are many ways to serve, whether overseas or locally: Witness to a neighbor. Donate to a local food bank. Sign up to build houses or do relief work. We can do *something*. On our own we might struggle to make an impact, but working together, the church can accomplish a lot. I hope we pray. I hope we care. I hope we act. I hope our hearts are moved outside of ourselves so that we make a difference for the Lord in this world. Then here's the added bonus: when we focus our attention on loving others, it helps us out of our own caves.

David understood this. Through all his confusion, depression and guilt, he had a heart that was soft enough to be touched by Keilah's plight. All David did was open himself to be used by God again. He told the Lord that he was ready to get back into whatever plan God had for his life, and God gave him new direction and new hope.

Prayer Gets Us Out of Our Caves

It's true that caring for others is essential for getting our focus off ourselves, but it's important for us to help people for the right reason. I'm not saying that we should overanalyze compassion; God *always* wants us to show love and mercy to others. But God can use us best when we ask Him how we fit into the process He already has for redeeming creation. To do that we have to find out God's plan.

When David heard about what was happening in Keilah, he didn't immediately jump to his feet, draw his sword and take off running. His immediate response was to pray. He asked God if he should help the people of Keilah (the answer was yes), and then he asked the Lord to verify that he really was doing the right thing. It's a good thing he did, because when the other men around David voiced their fears, David could stand firm on what the Lord had told him: "Arise, go down to Keilah, for I will give the Philistines into your hand" (1 Sam. 23:4). What a promise! David obeyed and went to fight the Philistines. He dealt them a great blow, carried off their livestock and saved the inhabitants of Keilah. Thank God that when He makes a promise, He keeps it!

Let me rewind for a minute. Remember how David had visited Ahimelech the priest as he fled from Saul and eaten some showbread? Saul had responded angrily to Ahimelech's kindness and had him and all the priests and their families killed. Abiathar, the son of Ahimelech, was the only one to survive the massacre at Nob, and he had fled to hide out with David in the cave. Now, as David went to Keilah, Abiathar went with him, and he brought an ephod with him. An ephod was a long vest that the priests wore; it had twelve jewels on it to represent the twelve tribes of Israel, and it was used to help determine God's will.

Saul heard that David had gone to Keilah, and he thought, *I've got him right where I want him.* Saul ordered his people to go to battle at Keilah to besiege David and his men. David knew that Saul would use any means possible to bring him harm, so he told Abiathar to bring him the ephod, and once again David sought God's will. David prayed,

> O LORD, the God of Israel, your servant has surely heard that Saul seeks to come to Keilah, to destroy the city on my account. Will the men of Keilah surrender me into his hand? Will Saul come down, as your servant has heard? O LORD, the God of Israel, please tell your servant. (23:10–11)

I like the words "please tell your servant," because they reveal that David's heart was once again tuned to serve and that he was genuinely seeking the Lord's will.

God told David that Saul would indeed come to Keilah and that the men of the town would turn him over into Saul's hands. Scary news. So David and his six hundred men (David sure knew how to attract a crowd!) scattered across the countryside. When Saul heard that David had escaped from Keilah, he cancelled the attack on the city. David hid in the hill country, "and Saul sought him every day, but God did not give him into his hand" (23:14).

What I love about the actions in this chapter is that they revolve around David's prayers. Going to fight in Keilah was not a natural response to the problem, in light of David's circumstances; in First Samuel 23:3, the other men told David that it was crazy to take on the Philistines. But David asked God what he was to do, and God told him to go, so he went. Then God told him to fight, so he fought. Then God told him to get out, so he left. David surrendered the entire matter to prayer.

The only way we're going to hear from God and get out of our caves is to talk to Him. This sounds obvious, but it isn't always a natural response to the problems we face. Regardless, biblical precedent tells us that the way to follow God's process and plan for our lives is to ask Him how to do things. Abraham asked God what he should do, and God directed him and made him the father of many nations. Moses consulted God every step of the way in his confrontations with Pharaoh, and God told him what to say. Jesus Christ—God in the flesh—went into the wilderness to pray and to find out what the Father wanted Him to do, and guess what? God spoke to Him. Prayer is a tried-and-true method for hearing from God.

And prayer works just as powerfully today as it did in biblical times. One of my friend's sons who is in his early twenties recently suffered a nervous breakdown. Over the past few years, this young man had been diagnosed with this and that, and the more things that went wrong for him, the more depressed he got. He finally told his parents that he hated them and never wanted to see them again, and his parents were afraid that he might try to kill himself. My friend told me that as he and his wife were hiding all their knives and anything that could be used as a weapon, he thought, *How did we get here? How did we go wrong?* My friend was in a cave. So he and his wife turned to God. One whole night they prayed, lying on the floor on their faces, crying out to God to show them what to do. And God is working. God is providing direction in that situation.

Listening Gets Us Out of Our Caves

Maybe it's obvious that when we ask God to speak to us, we also have to listen for His answer, but sometimes we rush from prayer right back into whatever we feel like doing. Because God doesn't typically tell us what to do audibly, we need to actively watch and long for His plans to unfold, and we need to listen for His truth to come to us through the insight of other believers.

When we follow Christ's command to love others, the people we show love to will invest back into us. (Once again involvement with other people help us get out of caves!) While David was hiding out in the wilderness, Jonathan—David's buddy and Saul's son—came to find him and told him, "Do not fear, for the hand of Saul my father shall not find you. You shall be king over Israel, and I shall be next to you. Saul my father also knows this" (1 Sam. 23:17). Jonathan, the genealogical heir to the throne, came to find David to give him his support and to encourage him. When Jonathan said, "I'll be next to you," he was telling David that he had his back, that he was on David's side. Talk about a way to strengthen David's resolve to trust the Lord!

As I mentioned in an earlier chapter, God doesn't always bring answers straight to us. Sometimes He brings them through a brother or sister in Christ who speaks God's Word to us—someone who, as Jonathan did for David in First Samuel 23:16, strengthens our hand in the Lord. Maybe the reason we don't hear from the Lord at times is because we're not open to hearing God's wisdom spoken through a fellow believer. Maybe we're not placing ourselves in relationships or environments in which someone can help us hear from the Lord.

To feel uncertain, all we have to do is commiserate with fearful people. To be negative all the time, we just have to associate with pessimists. If we want to learn to trust God, we have to associate with other people who trust God, people who trust that He's working even when they can't quite see what He's doing. This is the "secret" to developing correct spiritual perspective and to hearing what the Lord is saying to us.

Are You Living in a Cave?

When we read the Bible, we learn that even great men of God like David struggled to follow God. Sometimes these men wandered from the truth and got kind of depressed. David battled guilt and self-absorption. Things looked bad for David for a while, but (spoiler alert!) God turned things around for him. I say this because it's important to remember that God never forgets us—even when we're feeling lost and are stuck in one of life's depressing caves. God remembered David, and He remembers us.

Often when we become depressed and confused, we pull into ourselves. We seek a way to protect ourselves from the cruel outside world, which damages us emotionally and spiritually. Instead, when we end up in dark place, we should ask God to forgive us for whatever brought us there. Then we need to work to get out. To be set free and to get right with God, we have to obey whatever God tells us to do. When we break free from our natural way of thinking and begin to see life as God sees it, we move away from our caves of fear and insecurity.

One thing I hope we can learn from David is how to get out of our caves. David didn't initially react well when things in his life took a turn for the worse, but the good news is that he didn't stay in the cave of Adullam, feeling uncertain and afraid. Instead David worked to get back on the right track, and I pray that his story would speak to us and teach us how we too can break into the joy of God's design. David's example offers several steps to help us get out of a place of despair or anger and back into the process and plan that God has for us.

God's Process

So what should we do when we're in a cave? The worst thing we can do is try to pull ourselves up by our own bootstraps to get ourselves back in the game. The best thing we can do is to pray.

I repeat, because this is so important: we need to set aside time to pray. Prayer can mean a lot of different things; I'm not saying that we need to sit in a quiet room and have a conversation with God in our heads. Our prayer time might last ten minutes or it might last two hours, but we need to get it done with God. We need to talk our problems through until we have peace.

Sometimes when I'm having trouble verbalizing what I'm feeling, I try writing a letter to God; sometimes getting my thoughts down on paper helps me identify why I'm struggling. Basically, we need to do whatever it takes to hear from God. We need to honestly speak to God—which might involve crying, laughing, screaming, whatever—and wait for an answer from Him. We have to pray until we're out of the cave, and then—just to switch it up a little—pray some more.

God is the only One who knows what's best for us, so God has to be the One to direct us. And when God gives us an answer, we need to act on it. Every time we find ourselves asking, "Now what?" we need to get back on our faces before the Lord. Even when we can't see where the steps are leading, we need to keep following and keep praying and keep trusting God with each step.

I've been the pastor at my church in New Jersey for thirty-two years now, and we've had to humble ourselves and pray and wait to hear from God countless times. We all hit strategic points in our lives when we need to pray and wait on a specific word from the Lord. The "normal" Christian life involves continually asking God to lead us and to show us each new step. If we don't do this, we get stuck in the cave of despair and confusion again and again.

Here's another thing: reading and knowing the Word is fundamental to producing faith and trust, but sometimes just knowing what God says isn't enough to transform our attitude. Seeing other Christians living out God's truth has had a huge impact on my faith. When I observe brothers and sisters applying God's Word to their lives, when I learn from people's past mistakes and pray in faith and receive answers through prayer, it's then that my own faith is strengthened. It's then that my spiritual perspectives are broadened and deepened. It's then that my walk with God takes on new meaning and hope.

I believe God wants to speak to us through other people—through brothers and sisters in Christ, not just through pastors. Are we listening? Are we actively seeking to hear from the Lord not just in our personal prayer times but in our social interactions? Are we in relationship with people who encourage us in the faith and who come alongside us to reassure us that we're doing the right thing by trusting and waiting on God?

The worldview that says life is what we make of it is wrong. Instead, we need to follow the one that God gives us in the Bible: God has placed us on this earth to be part of His mission. God will do amazing things if we allow Him to work out His processes through us.

Now is the time for us to get out of our dark caves. As a community of Christians, we need God to open our hearts to be touched by others' needs. Here are a few key steps for us to take to get our hearts back on the right track: (1) Pray through guilt from the past; talk it out with God. (2) Get into a place where God can speak to you through others. (3) Live in the expectation that God will bring you back on track. (4) Tell the Lord that you're responding to what He's done and what He's doing. Tell Him that you're all in. And then ask Him to get you out of your cave and back into the process of growth He has for you.

Let's pray:

Lord, thank You for being the Light that guides us out of our caves and into Your will. Teach us, Father, to be compassionate. Teach us to remain in a posture of prayer before You and then to listen to Your direction. In Jesus' name, amen.

CHAPTER NINE

DAVID, THE HUMAN TARGET: HOW TO RESPOND TO ATTACKS

1 Samuel 24, 26

Pastor Glenn Kantner

There is no wrong or treason in my hands. I have not sinned against you, though you hunt my life to take it.
1 Samuel 24:11

Even when our hearts are in sync with God's, we're going to face some struggles. David was a man after God's heart, but he ended up in some sticky situations. Part of faith is accepting that God is going to grow us in ways we don't understand. Part of trusting God's hand involves walking alongside Him through both the good and the bad.

Today God is still renewing this earth, establishing His eternal kingdom's ways of grace, mercy and love. We don't see much of those qualities in the world today, because Satan is still fighting to break relationships and cause animosity. The first step to right living is recognizing that the battle we're fighting is so much bigger than that quarrel we got into at work or the money the cashier at the grocery store cheated us out of. We're in the middle of a spiritual battle, and we're being targeted by the Enemy.

The fact that we are targeted because we are Christians

doesn't mean that God is punishing us. Rather, it means that Satan recognizes how God is using us and wants to manipulate others' sinful natures to try to distract us from our purpose. Take David for example. God had a plan to make David king, so Satan worked through Saul to try to thwart that plan. Saul's kingdom (of this earth) came against David's kingdom (of the Lord's purpose and will). It was precisely because David was striving to follow the Lord that he had to face some adversity.

In order for God's Spirit to work through us, we need to stand for Him—even when we're being targeted. That requires a big helping of His grace. Thankfully, all the elements we need to be able to respond to attacks with grace are found in First Samuel 24 and 26. Let's take a look.

David: Being Careful About Ourselves

When we find ourselves targeted, the first thing we need to do is be careful about ourselves. We want to remain in God's will as we respond to our aggressors. In chapter 24 David was hiding in a cave with four to five hundred of his men, and Saul was coming after him with three thousand. (Not exactly a fair fight.) But then nature called, and Saul went into a cave to relieve himself. He just so happened to pick, without knowing it, the very same cave that David was hiding in.

David's men stayed very quiet as Saul went to the bathroom, and David crept up and cut off the corner of Saul's garment. David's men wanted to kill Saul, but David wouldn't let them. After Saul left and was far enough away, David came out of the cave, held up the edge of the garment and pointed out to Saul that he'd had the chance to kill him. Saul recognized how narrowly he had escaped death. Extremely impressed by the grace David had shown to him, Saul promised to never hunt David again.

Of course, we know by this point that Saul's word wasn't

worth much. Two chapters later Saul came back, with three thousand choice men, to kill David. When night fell, Saul's men made camp. As king and commander, Saul got to sleep nearest the fire in the middle of the encampment. David and one of his men, Abishai, crept down into the camp and went past all the other soldiers, right up to Saul. Abishai wanted to kill Saul right then and there. He said, "This is the opportunity God has given us. Let's kill him and be done with it" But David said, "No. We can't do that" (see 26:8–11). Instead, David took Saul's spear and water jug, and he and Abishai crept back to their own camp. Daylight came, and David called to Saul once again—and he once again proved that he could have taken Saul's life but hadn't. Saul was again so surprised and thankful that he hardly knew how to respond. So he asked David for a favor, which we'll look at in just a bit.

But first I want to rewind to look more closely at the temptations David faced and the ways he carefully considered and handled them. The first temptation was posed by his own men: "The men of David said to him, 'Here is the day of which the LORD said to you, "Behold, I will give your enemy into your hand, and you shall do to him as it shall seem good to you"'" (24:4) The men's petition sounded scriptural, and I'm sure David had to admit that the circumstances were compelling. After all, God had promised to make him king. By this point David had been running from Saul for at least seven or eight years, which is a long time for him to have spent scrounging for food and watching over his shoulder for the guys who were out to kill him! David's men were likely tired of camping in the wilderness, so they reasoned that God must have brought the current king, Saul, into David's hands so he could kill him and ascend to the throne. That *had* to be God's will, right?

I know David wanted to sleep in a real bed, eat a good dinner and be Israel's king, as God had said he would be. He had to have been tempted to listen to what his men were saying, but it's clear from Scripture that those things were not first and foremost on his mind. Instead, David was focused on God's Word, and he checked what looked like God's will against Scriptural precedent. David knew the Old Testament teachings, including Exodus 22:28: "You shall not revile God, nor curse a ruler of your people." In order for David to kill Saul, he would have to dishonor him, and he knew that wouldn't be right. David wanted to please God more than anything—even more than he wanted to get out of the wilderness. So he was careful about himself. He was careful not to mistake serendipitous circumstances for the will of God.

Sometimes we get the idea that God wants us to be happy, so we decide that pain can't be part of His plan. It certainly wasn't true that pain was absent in David's situation, however. Now we *can* say that God had to be behind Saul "randomly" choosing the cave that David was hiding in. But God didn't bring Saul to David so that David could kill him; I think God had other reasons for this encounter. Saul had been operating within the rules of the kingdom of this earth: namely, do whatever is possible to get ahead. When David extended grace and mercy to him by not killing him, Saul was confronted by the kingdom of heaven, and it astounded him. Note Saul's response. He blessed David. Coming up against someone who was a reflection of God, Saul couldn't maintain his lust for murder. David's goodwill rubbed off on him a little.

When we follow God's purpose during times of attack, sticking to what He tells us to do in His Word, God's presence is shown to the people pursuing us, and they're astounded. They recognize that there's some unusual force at work that allows us to be gracious when we've been wronged. When we seek and test God's will and then act on it, we reveal to others a piece of God's kingdom in the here and now.

David was careful not to mistake God's will, and he was also careful to keep his conscience sharp. After David cut off a corner of Saul's robe, First Samuel says that "David's heart struck him" (24:5). He said, "The LORD forbid that I should do this thing to my lord, the LORD's anointed, to put out my hand against him, seeing he is the LORD's anointed" (24:6). Why did David get so upset over having made a little clothing alteration? Many biblical scholars believe that what David did by his action was symbolically state that Saul wasn't fit to be king. This bothered David and pricked at his heart, so he repented of what he had done, telling his men that he had acted wrongly. Then David encouraged his men to behave correctly and to spare Saul's life. David was careful to keep his conscience sharp by listening to it.

On the other hand, if David had ignored his conscience, he would have dulled it. Isn't that true for us as well? The more we overlook our conscience, refusing to listen to it, the duller it becomes. Then the next time our conscience pricks us, it's not as strong, and it is easier to ignore. And the next time, it's even easier. Finally our consciences get so beaten down that God gives us up to our selfish desires and leaves us without a good moral compass (see Rom. 1:18–32). The decisions we make reflect either our desire to rely on God and on His Word or our tendency to do whatever we feel like doing, without regard to the consequences. Like David, we need to be careful about the decisions of our heart. When we train ourselves to trust our trustworthy God, He shows us the best way to respond to those who are harassing us.

David: Being Careful About Other People

In addition to watching over his own heart, David was also careful to respond in the right way to the person who was pursuing him. David demonstrated a couple of key points for us. First we need to respect the other person, whether or not that person happens to be following God.

Verses 8–11 of First Samuel explain how David reverently revealed to Saul what had happened and what he had done. David called Saul "my lord the king"—words of recognition and honor. Then he bowed to the earth, paying homage to Saul's title. Most people would say Saul wasn't worthy of the honor David accounted to him. David, however, recognized that whether or not Saul was behaving in a way deserving of his rank, it was still his responsibility to show respect to his superior. Rather than giving in to his own emotions, David acted according to God's commands.

Let's bring this closer to home. If someone in authority over us—a supervisor or a law-enforcement officer or a committee head, for example—is targeting us, it's our responsibility to respect that person's office. For that matter, even someone we consider our equal deserves our respect. God made that person in His own image and gave him or her life. God's mark is on every person; therefore every human being—regardless of rank or religion—deserves to be respected.

I once heard a rather special lesson taught by a theology professor. One day he told his students, "Think of someone you dislike or who has hurt you and sketch that person's face on a piece of paper." He then had the students—one by one—pin their papers over a target he had attached to the classroom's corkboard. The students took turns throwing darts at their enemies, and they really got into it. It was clear that the students were releasing a lot of their pent up anger on those drawings; sometimes the papers were so torn up that the faces became indistinguishable. When everyone had had a turn, the professor asked the students to sit down. Then, without saying a word, he walked over to the target and undid the thumbtacks holding it to the board. Behind the target was a picture of Jesus Christ, marred by holes from hundreds of darts. The professor turned to the group and said, "I assure you that when you did this to one of the least of these my brothers and sisters, you were doing it to me" (see Matt. 25:40). Nothing more needed to be said.

When we hurt others, we hurt Christ. If for no other reason, we should strive for His sake to love those around us, including our enemies.

In addition to respecting Saul's authority, David was also careful to communicate truth to him. He said, "See, my father, see the corner of your robe in my hand. For by the fact that I cut off the corner of your robe and did not kill you, you may know and see that there is no wrong or treason in my hands. I have not sinned against you, though you hunt my life to take it" (24:11). David here provided evidence—almost as if he was in a courtroom, proving why he was innocent and shouldn't be killed. He showed Saul the garment he had taken as proof that he could have killed Saul; he made Saul an eyewitness to his upstanding nature. Whenever Saul looked down at his robe after this incident, he would be confronted with God's graciousness.

Then, in First Samuel 26:18, David asked Saul what he had done to make Saul come after him. That was a good question. We too should ask those who have wronged us if we have cause them hurt, because sometimes, when someone is upset with us and targeting us, we've missed something. None of us are perfect individuals; we all make mistakes. So when we find ourselves targeted, we need to be humble and ask what we might have done wrong. We're at least 1 percent at fault in every disagreement, and we need to own up to that 1 percent, as small as it might be. We need to take care to respect others and to seek opportunities to provide them with truth as well as evidence of that truth.

There's one more important piece to being careful with those who target us. David doesn't exemplify this point, but Jesus does. Christ tells us, "Love your enemies, do good to those who hate you, bless those who curse you, pray for those who abuse you" (Luke 6:27–28). It's a challenge for us to love and ask for blessings on those who have wronged us; it's not easy to pray for those who have hurt us. But Christ didn't say this to hear Himself talk; He gave us this instruction for our own benefit and for the benefit of others. And Jesus not only taught this; He lived it. For the men who beat Him and put Him on a cross to die, Jesus prayed, "Father, forgive them, for they know not what they do" (Luke 23:34).

David: Being Careful About God

A relationship between people is only healthy when God is involved, so we need to be careful about Him as well when we are interacting with people who are targeting us. Again, David did this the right way. First, he was careful to leave the punishment to God. In First Samuel 24:12 David told Saul, "May the LORD judge between me and you, may the LORD avenge me against you, but my hand shall not be against you." David spoke God's truth into the situation, reminding Saul that one day God would judge him for all the wrong he had done. Leaving justice to the Lord, David freed himself from bitterness and from the need to get back at Saul.

If David had avenged himself, he would have overstepped his boundaries. Romans 12:19 tells us, "Behold, never avenge yourselves, but leave it to the wrath of God, for it is written, 'Vengeance is mine, I will repay, says the Lord.'" We have this verse to remind us that it's not up to us to deal out punishment. Now David obviously didn't have the writings of the New Testament, but he knew that if he went for revenge, he would have to answer to God. He asked Abishai, "Who can put out his hand against the LORD's anointed and be guiltless?" (1 Sam. 26:9) David was careful not to cross God, trusting that it was the Lord's responsibility to handle Saul. David went on to tell Abishai that the Lord Himself would deal with Saul either by striking him with a malady, sending him to die in battle or allowing him to live to a ripe old age and then making him answer for the wrongs of his life after death (see 26:10). David was at peace, no matter what the outcome, because he knew that the Lord would bring justice to the situation.

Second, in addition to allowing God to do the punishing, David was careful to forgive Saul in the way that God tells us to forgive. When Saul discovered that David had spared his life, he was so thankful that he pronounced a blessing on David, asking the Lord to reward him for showing him kindness. Then Saul continued, "I know that you shall surely be king, and that the kingdom of Israel shall be established in your hands. Swear to me therefore by the LORD that you will not cut off my offspring after me, and that you will not destroy my name out of my father's house" (24:20–21).

Saul was finally admitting that he knew David would one day be king; he got on his knees before the man he had been plotting to kill and asked him for a favor. It was common in Saul's days for a new king to kill the extended family of the old king so that there wouldn't be any threat to his throne. David showed forgiveness in promising Saul that he would allow his descendents to live. He was very gracious to grant Saul's request to never harm him or his family.

After David made his promise to Saul, Saul went home, but David and his men went to the stronghold where he had been staying (see 23:14, 29; 24:22). Why didn't David go to the palace now that Saul had admitted that David would be king? David had forgiven Saul freely, but he still didn't trust him. Too many times before Saul had promised to stop pursuing David and then, with his very next breath, he had thrown a spear at him. David let precedent speak for itself; he saved himself from bitterness by forgiving Saul, but he continued to be careful and wise in the relationship.

God's Amazing Grace

I personally struggle a lot with the inhumanity of some humans to others. When people attack me and others whom I love, it gives me pause. But God has called us to love radically—even (or perhaps especially) when we're the ones being targeted. I hesitate to share the story I'm about to tell, because it's hard for those of us who live in stable, free countries to relate to the horrific treatment it describes, but I think it offers a strong example of faith under attack. So let's go back in time to a courtroom trial in South Africa.

A frail, black woman, over seventy years old, slowly stood to face several white police officers. One of the officers, Mr. Vanderbrook, has just been tried and found guilty of murdering the two men closest to this woman. Mr. Vanderbrook had come to the woman's house and shot her son point-blank, then he and the other officers had partied as they burned the young man's body. Several years later, Mr. Vanderbrook and his cohorts returned and kidnapped the woman's husband. For months the woman heard nothing about his whereabouts, until one night Mr. Vanderbrook came to fetch her. He took her down to the riverbank, where her husband lay on a pile of wood, bound and beaten but still strong in spirit. As Mr. Vanderbrook and the other officers poured gasoline over his body and set him on fire, his wife heard him utter, "Father, forgive them."

As the woman stood in the courtroom, a member of South Africa's Truth and Reconciliation Commission turned to her and asked, "How would you like justice to be done?" I ask myself what I would have done to a man who so brutally and mockingly destroyed my family, and I'm not sure I could have responded with the grace this woman did. Here is what she said: "I want three things. First, I would like to be taken back to the riverbed where my husband was burned so I can gather some of his ashes and give him a decent burial. Second, because I have no family left, I would like Mr. Vanderbrook to come spend a day with me, twice a month, in my home in the ghetto. That way I can love him with the love I have left in the way I would love my family if they were still here. Third, I would like Mr.

Vanderbrook to know that I offer him my forgiveness, because Jesus Christ died to forgive. Would someone please help me across this courtroom so I can embrace Mr. Vanderbrook and let him know that he's truly forgiven?"[1] As the court assistants came to lead the elderly woman over to Mr. Vanderbrook, he fainted, overwhelmed by what he had heard. As he struggled to regain consciousness, those in the courtroom—friends, family and neighbors who were all victims of decades of oppression and injustice—began to softly but assuredly sing, "Amazing grace, how sweet the sound, that saved a wretch like me . . ."

I have a hard time finding room in my heart to forgive Mr. Vanderbrook. And I think there's a good reason why I can't: God has not given me the grace to do such a thing, because I'm not facing that situation. God gives us the grace to face our own unique circumstances. Whenever we're pursued, whenever others are coming after us because of our faith in Christ, God's grace is available to us. Mr. Vanderbrook was given a glimpse of the kingdom of heaven in that courtroom, and it was more than he could stand. That's what happens when we choose to respond to those who persecute us with grace and mercy. We have to fight our inclination to beat others down when they hurt or offend us. It's God's intent that wherever we go, whatever we do, we help people see a picture of what the kingdom of heaven is really like. That's what we're designed to do. When people catch a glimpse of real truth, hope and love, they're astounded. They can't believe that people would really live this way, God's way.

Giving grace glorifies God, and it awards us peace. But despite all its positives, because grace is something divine, it doesn't come naturally to us to extend it to others—especially when people are targeting us with animosity and harsh actions—anything from being bullied by a brother or sister to dealing with a fellow employee who has it in for us. When someone is trying to run us into the ground, it's difficult to do our best to help that person, yet that's what the Bible tells us to do:

If your enemy is hungry, give him bread to eat,
    and if he is thirsty, give him water to drink,
for you will heap burning coals on his head,
    and the LORD will reward you. (Prov. 25:21–22)

This verse doesn't just mean that we should provide for our enemies' physical needs; it's equally important to care for their emotional and spiritual wellbeing. This is especially challenging for us when we have a me-first attitude instead of a God-first, others-second, me-third attitude.

Attacks aren't always physically obvious. Maybe a guy is teased and harassed because he won't go out to the bars and strip clubs with the other guys. Maybe a lady has another woman maneuvering for her job. Maybe a community emotionally targets a family, spreading rumors about them just because they're Christians. Sometimes just being who God made us to be is going to turn us into targets. Second Timothy 3:12 promises, "All who desire to live a godly life in Christ Jesus *will be persecuted.*" If we're living for Jesus, we're going to be targeted, so we had better learn the godly way to handle it.

Trash in Our Baskets

Psalm 37:8 tells us, "Refrain from anger, and forsake wrath! Fret not yourself; it tends only to evil." Being preoccupied with our hurts will only lead to evil; it won't do us any good. We can say that the person who's targeting us doesn't deserve grace, but remember—we don't deserve God's forgiveness either.

I heard about a four-year-old who misunderstood the part of the Lord's prayer that says, "Forgive us our trespasses as we forgive those who trespass against us." He recited the prayer this way: "Forgive us our trash baskets as we forgive those who put trash in our baskets." I rather like that version, because it's true, isn't it? People put trash in our baskets, running us into the ground and hurting us. Cuts and scrapes heal pretty quickly, but emotional hurts are hard to forgive. Our minds remember the pain, and they keep replaying events over and over and over again. There's a word for that: *resentment*. The word "resentment" comes from a root meaning "to cut again." Every time we replay something in our minds that someone has done against us rather than forgiving that person, it's like we're reopening the wound, refreshing the pain. The way of forgiveness is the way of letting go. If we don't release our hurts, we'll never be all that God intends us to be. It's in our best interest to let Him into our relationship with the person who has hurt us so that we can walk in His freedom.

We access God's grace by being careful about ourselves and our consciences, by being careful about others and showing them respect and by being careful about God—careful to forgive as He tells us to forgive, to pray for our enemies and to leave vengeance up to the Lord. When we take the steps to do these things, we will find true peace.

We need to ask the Lord to help us reflect His kingdom to those around us. I hope we will become more like David—careful in our relationships and quick to forgive. I pray that even as we struggle with being targeted, we will show grace and mercy to those who persecute us. I pray that our offenders will be so astonished by our treatment of them that they will be driven to the God of grace.

Let's pray:

Heavenly Father, we thank You for extending Your incredible grace to us. Give us the strength and the heart to extend that same grace to those who hurt us. In Jesus' name, amen.

CHAPTER TEN

DAVID GETS MAD:
HOW TO HANDLE ANGER

1 Samuel 25

Pastor Marty Berglund

Now David had said, "Surely in vain have I guarded all that this fellow has in the wilderness, so that nothing was missed of all that belonged to him, and he has returned me evil for good. God do so to the enemies of David and more also, if by morning I leave so much as one male of all who belong to him."
1 Samuel 25:21–22

When we've been targeted, it's easy for us to grow bitter and angry about our situation. Even though David was defined as a man after God's own heart, he wasn't perfect. He was filled with unrighteous anger from time to time, and it made him act on improper impulses. By examining David's anger, we can discern ways to protect our own hearts from the destructive influences of anger and resentment. Rather than maliciously beating others into the ground emotionally, God desires that we choose to love others and treat them with respect.

Years ago, when I was in seminary, I had a professor named Dr. Duane Litfin. He'd done extensive research on power and authority, and he taught that in any relationship there is always one person ruling and one being ruled. This led him to the astounding discovery that no ruler has any power other than that which those under him have allowed . A government, for example, can only rule if its citizens submit to its authority and don't rebel. A teacher can only teach his or her students if they submit to being taught. This corresponds with what the Bible suggests: God is the ultimate ruler, but we human beings are still free to make our own choices. Just as in any over-under relationship, we have to choose to accept Christ as Lord over our life.

That means that we also have the ability to choose wrongly. We can submit ourselves to anger or greed or fear or lust. We don't typically think that we have an active role in allowing ourselves to become upset or envious, yet we do allow these emotions to rule us and to have a strong impact on our decisions and actions.

In life we're bound to confront people and situations that will anger us, so we need to learn to let go of our irritation and desire for revenge. That's what David teaches us in First Samuel 25, a dramatic chapter that contains all the necessary components of a blockbuster movie—betrayal, rage and redemption. In addition to its compelling plot, chapter 25 coaches us to choose to submit to God and to allow Him to be Lord over everything in our lives.

Getting the Right Perspective

Here's the short version of First Samuel 25: As David and his men traveled, they came across Nabal's sheep and sheepherders. In those days it was common for marauding tribes of thieves to steal sheep. Without being asked, David and his men voluntarily watched out for Nabal's sheep and his shepherds. While they were watching over them, not one sheep went missing, and the shepherds were cared for.

When sheep-sheering time came, David sent a couple of his men to Nabal to report that he and his men had helped him out and to ask if Nabal would help them out now. That might sound a little shady, but I promise, this was nothing like a mafia deal; it was more like getting a tip. It's customary to give a little something to someone who has helped us out. Unfortunately, however, Nabal was not a very well-behaved man, so he sent David's men back with the reply, "Who is David that I should give him a handout? I don't owe you guys anything. Scat!" (see 25:10–11). When David's men reported back to him, he became angry and essentially declared war on Nabal, vowing to kill every last man on Nabal's property.

In the meantime, Nabal's wife, Abigail, heard from the servants what her husband had done. Without telling Nabal she collected a peace offering of various foods and took it to David and his men. Thanks to Abigail's quick thinking and her plea, which we'll look at in due time, David's wrath cooled, and he turned back from his war route. God then struck down Nabal, and David married Abigail. That's the basic synopsis, but there are obviously a lot of details that need to be filled in.

I want to look at David's reaction to Nabal's insult. The book of First Samuel has not, up until this point, portrayed David as an angry man. When Saul made David jump through hoops to marry his daughter, David did what was asked of him without complaining. When Saul threw a spear at David, David dodged the weapon and ran. When Saul hunted him down, David still showed him respect. But chapter 25 shows us that David was a man who was still liable to lose his temper.

Often we can keep our anger under control when someone offends us in private, but the second we're publicly insulted, we get furious. This is what happened to David. David's sense of entitlement and pride made him livid when Nabal refused to act according to custom and provide for David and his men.

Thankfully, Abigail came along and redeemed the situation. Abigail said to David, "Blame me for what happened, because I should have been there when your boys came. Nabal is a fool, but it would be wrong for you to kill all Nabal's men in seeking revenge. May the Lord keep you!" (see 25:24–26). Abigail told David that holding a grudge against Nabal wasn't worth hurting his reputation or his heart.

The main point of her argument is found in verse 28: "Please forgive the trespass of your servant. For the LORD will certainly make my lord a sure house, because my lord is fighting the battles of the LORD, and evil shall not be found in you so long as you live." Abigail showed David that he was focused on the wrong thing. She encouraged him to look at how the Lord was going to use him and bless him rather than to think of how he could avenge himself of a minor offense. Abigail is the hero of First Samuel 25, because in showing David how to trade his clouded perspective for a godly one, she saved many innocent lives.

Refuse to Seek Revenge

After refreshing David's perspective, Abigail cautioned him against vengeance. David was upset that Nabal had returned him evil for good (see Prov. 17:3)—coldly turning David away after he had freely offered his services of protection. So David basically vowed to kill everyone remotely connected with Nabal (see 1 Sam. 25:22). David's reaction was pretty extreme. Yet we often operate this way as well, justifying our revenge from childhood on with complaints like "He hit me first" or "She started it." This way of laying blame to protect ourselves isn't right. The old retribution laws of Exodus 21:23–25—"an eye for an eye and a tooth for a tooth"—were redefined by Christ in Matthew 5:38–42, verses that urge us to compassion, forgiveness and grace.

Abigail revealed to David that his way of seeking revenge wasn't right, and she reminded him to trust the Lord to handle his enemies. I love the imagery of God wrapping David in His loving care that Abigail used: "If men rise up to pursue you and to seek your life, the life of my lord shall be bound in the bundle of the living in the care of the LORD your God. And the lives of your enemies He shall sling out as from the hollow of a sling" (1 Sam. 25:29). Abigail told David that if he would just decide to forgive Nabal, the Lord would handle the situation and sustain David.

No matter how we've been wronged, it's not up to us to seek revenge. As we noted earlier, Romans 12:19 reminds us of the Lord's words from Deuteronomy 32:25: "Beloved, never avenge yourselves, but leave it to the wrath of God, for it is written, 'Vengeance is mine, I will repay, says the Lord.'" When we try to avenge the wrongs we've suffered, we effectively overstep our boundaries and try to do God's job. Anger is no excuse for unjust retribution. Take a step back and leave it to the Lord.

In his book *Love & Respect*, Dr. Emerson Eggerichs talks about something he calls the crazy cycle. He says that marriages can get stuck in a loop of "He said," "She said," "He did this," "She did that," until one member of the party decides to stop seeking revenge and trying to prove that he or she is right. The relationship begins to be restored when someone submits to the care of the Lord—just as Abigail advised David to do.

How did Abigail become so wise? How did she know that David needed to turn his situation over to the Lord rather than seek vengeance on his own? Abigail had lived her entire married life with Nabal, a man who was ruthless and foolish, and she had learned that the best way to survive, the only way to survive, was to give everything over to the Lord's care. I believe Abigail's words had such a strong impact on David because she was essentially sharing her own testimony with him. While she couldn't control what Nabal said or did, she could control her reactions; she could choose to submit to God instead of becoming upset or vengeful.

Abigail told David to stop trying to even the score. She told him to be the bigger person and to be merciful. And sure enough, when David gave his anger over to the Lord, God handled his situation. After Nabal sobered up, Abigail told him what David had been planning to do and what she had done. First Samuel 25:37 says that Nabal's "heart died within him, and he became as a stone"; he had what appears to be a stroke. Ten days later he died. Nabal was struck down, and David didn't have to dirty his hands or sully his heart.

Here's the applicable lesson: leave revenge to the Lord.

Refuse to Allow Anger to Deafen Us to God's Message

David could have ignored Abigail's wisdom, writing her off as the wife of a fool. But after hearing Abigail out, David looked at her and said, "Blessed be the LORD, the God of Israel, who sent you this day to meet me! Blessed be your discretion, and blessed be you, who have kept me this day from bloodguilt and from avenging myself with my own hand!" (25:32–33). David really *listened* to what Abigail was saying, and he believed God had sent her to save him from doing something stupid! It's important never to allow anger to close us off to wisdom.

But how did David hear God speak through a woman he had never met before? I propose that it's because he knew the Lord's voice so well. Throughout his lifetime David had heard the Lord speak many times. He had studied the Scriptures. He had lived in close communion with God, praying and listening for God's response.

To hear God we have to become accustomed to the way He speaks. Knowing God's voice is similar to a dog knowing its master's voice; it is part intuition and part training. My father was a Marine in World War II, and when he was stationed in the Philippines, he trained dogs to sniff out landmines. Dad really got to know those dogs, because he spent eight, ten, twelve hours a day with them. When I was growing up, I got to see Dad's dog-training abilities firsthand. We had Labradors that Dad would train with signals and one-word commands. Eventually he would move from commands to just talking normally to the dog, and the dog would respond. Instead of saying "Sit!" Dad would ask, "Why don't you go over there and sit down?" and the dog would do it. He could talk to those dogs like humans, and they would do whatever he asked. Why? Bhose dogs knew my Dad's voice so well from the time they had spent together.

It's the same with us and the Lord. We learn the Lord's voice by spending time in His Word and by talking with Him. We learn what He sounds like and the kinds of things He asks from us. Then, when we hear a preacher teaching or a friend speaking a word into our lives, we're able to discern whether or not the Lord is speaking through them. We have to get used to listening to God so that He can speak to us through someone else when we've reached the end of our rope and are feeling wrathful.

That's how it was with David. When Abigail confronted him, he recognized that she was speaking the Lord's truth to him. Her wisdom made him realize that he had gone off in his own, unholy direction, and he repented. He thanked the Lord for sending Abigail to save him from making a terrible mistake.

Moving Past the Past

Countless people have come to me for counseling and have raged on and on about how awfully someone else has treated them. The best thing I can do for those people is to tell them to stop thinking about the other person's actions and to start focusing on the Lord. I've seen lives ruined by a fixation on something that someone said or did in the past.

I have a good friend named Chuck who grew up in West Virginia. He has a brother named Buck, and Buck and Chuck (yes, those are their real names) had a harsh father who was a drill sergeant in World War II. Their dad passed away a long time ago, but Buck still hates his father today, despising him for all the hurt and emotional abuse he put him through. Chuck, on the other hand, honors his dad and remembers him with love.

Chuck and Buck had the same father, who treated them the same way, but they chose to respond to their dad's treatment with very different attitudes. Chuck chose to forgive his dad, accepting that his father had done his best to raise his sons to be tough. Chuck got married to a great lady and now has two wonderful kids. Buck, however, has been married two or three times and has had all sorts of controversies and difficulties with his children. Over the years I've seen the lives of these two men grow and change, and it's clear to me that one guy forgave and the other held a grudge. One looked to the Lord to redeem his situation, and the other fixated on all the wrong that had been done to him.

If we're stuck stewing about something that has happened in our past, something has to change. There's no better time than right this instant to pull our focus away from our sense of hurt and injustice and look to the Lord. I hope Abigail's words resonate in our hearts too, convincing us to stop thinking and worrying about what other people have done to us. We have the freedom to choose the things that occupy our thought life. We have the ability to move through the haze of bitterness and anger and to allow the Lord to wash away whatever is troubling our heart so that we can more clearly see His purposes for our life.

Freedom Awaits

Are we open to hearing from the messengers that the Lord sends our way, or have we closed our ears in frustration? Are we willing to break the cycle of retribution and revenge and to surrender our hurt and sense of injustice to God? If we're fixated on something or someone that is ruining our life, we need to change our focus. We need to look at what God's Word has to say and then make the difficult choice to leave revenge to the Lord.

If anger is ruling us, the Lord is not truly our Lord: "If anyone says, 'I love God,' and hates his brother, he is a liar" (1

John 4:20). If we're carrying a grudge or are angry with someone for they way they've hurt us, we're failing to love the Lord. I know that sounds harsh, but it's biblical truth. There's only room for one lord of our life; is it *the* Lord?

God knows how others have hurt us; He knows what they've said and what they've done. He also knows how we feel about those people. He knows every last awful, unspeakable thought that's crossed our mind. Because He already knows everything, we can confess to Him how we're feeling and can talk (or yell) our anger out with God. Even if the person we're dealing with is foolish, wrong or even evil, it's not our responsibility to fix the situation, because the real battle is between that person and God. All we need to do is to ask the Lord to forgive us and to help us, like David did, and to make the choice not to get even. We can turn away from anger and revenge and ask God to help us forgive whoever has wronged us.

I pray that God will give us the strength and power to let go—to look to Him instead of at how we've been wronged. God *will* rescue us from our anger. He's waiting to lift the burden and to give us freedom.

Let's pray:

Lord, forgive us for allowing our anger to become a stronghold in our lives. Thank You for revealing to us the proper way of handling our frustrations and for the freedom that comes when we submit all our emotions to You. Amen

CHAPTER ELEVEN

DAVID FENDS FOR HIMSELF:
LEARNING TO WAIT ON GOD

1 Samuel 27–30

Pastor Glenn Kantner

How long, O LORD? Will you forget me forever?
How long will you hide your face from me?
Psalm 13:1

We often want God's best, but we don't want to wait for it. We want all His blessings, and we want them right now. And yet we spend much of our lives waiting for other things— waiting in line at the grocery store, waiting for a ride at an amusement park, waiting for the weekend to arrive. David went through a different, a longer, kind of waiting. He spent over ten years running from Saul and waiting for God to make good on His promises to him. David's waiting was akin to waiting for the right mate to come along or for an illness to recede or for a career to pick up.

The problem we have is that when we think we've waited for something long enough, we start getting tired and doubting that we'll ever see an outcome to all those hours of anticipation. Maybe we feel tempted to tell God that we've had enough of trusting Him for an outcome, and we resolve to get on with our lives, to move out on our own. I'm afraid that's what David did on numerous occasions. But when we do that, we discover what David discovered: there's something far worse than waiting, and it's *not* waiting.

The Wrong Kind of Waiting

All of David's hard days and bouts of anger and desperation ultimately taught him the importance of waiting on God:

> Wait for the LORD and keep his way,
>   and he will exalt you to inherit the land;
>   you will look on when the wicked are cut off. (Ps. 37:34)

David hadn't just heard that God would come through for him; he had seen it. He had also seen how disastrous going his own way could be, so he trained his heart to hold out for God's best instead of pushing ahead with his own plans. The only problem is that David wasn't so good at waiting. He went through seasons of trusting God, but he was still in a long process of getting his heart into the right place.

Remember back in First Samuel 26 when David spared Saul's life for the second time? Well, right after that, in chapter 27, David's whole situation really disintegrated. Even though Saul had promised not to pursue David anymore, David knew that he couldn't trust Saul to keep his word, and he was tired. He thought, "Now I shall perish one day by the hand of Saul. There is nothing better for me than that I should escape to the land of the Philistines. Then Saul will despair of seeking me any longer within the borders of Israel, and I shall escape out of his hand" (27:1). So, without consulting God (apparently he hadn't learned his lesson!), David decided to take care of his situation, and he went down to live in the Philistines' territory.

Sounds familiar, doesn't it? The last time David had gone there, he'd had to pretend to be insane to keep the Philistines from killing him (see 21:13). This time David took six hundred men with him, and King Achish accepted him. (Mindboggling that he let him in, right? But we'll talk about that later.) David and his buddies were given a town to live in, and Achish began to trust David.

From this snippet of the story, it may seem as if David's plans were succeeding. But success looks different from the perspective of a lifetime than it does in the moment. David's actions ended up being very damaging. When God has us in a place of waiting, but we decide to plow forward, there are serious consequences. We often have trouble waiting, just as David did, and we need to recognize and avoid the things in our lives that encourage us to blindly move ahead without paying heed to God's plan.

I want to look at *why* David ended up going his own way in the first place, because I think we're prone to do some of the same things that he did in our own lives. David had been running from Saul for about a decade when he got tired of constantly looking over his shoulder and being on his guard. He didn't just wake up one day and decide he was done waiting; he did several things that led to his decision to take matters into his own hands.

Don't Lose Sight of the Truth

First of all, David justified his actions by lying to himself: Remember, "David said in his heart, 'Now I shall perish one day by the hand of Saul'" (1 Sam. 27:1). Where did he get that idea? God had certainly never told David such a thing. I believe that statement came from David's fear. He knew that Saul would never give up coming after him, and he thought that even though he had been fortunate up until that point, sooner or later Saul was bound to get him. David got caught up in the past ten years' circumstances, and those circumstances began to appear more powerful to him than God's promise.

The honest-to-goodness truth, however, was that God had

told David that he would be king. Yet David convinced himself Saul was going to kill him; he lost sight of the truth and believed the lie:

> How long, O LORD? Will you forget me forever?
> > How long will you hide your face from me?
> How long must I take counsel in my soul
> > and have sorrow in my heart all the day?
> How long shall my enemy be exalted over me? (Ps. 13:1–2)

David felt as if God had forgotten Him, and that agonized him.

Maybe we could write a psalm similar to David's. Would ours read, "How long? How long, O Lord, must I struggle with this illness?" Or, "How long? How long, O Lord, must I struggle to raise these kids alone?" The list goes on: "How long must I wait for my finances to get straightened out?" "How long must I suffer in this broken relationship?" It's not wrong for us to ask the Lord questions, but it is wrong for us to allow ourselves to drown in self-pity, focusing on all our questions and on all the things that are wrong. Sometimes we miss God's promises because we blot them out with doubt and with fear of our circumstances. Our questions grow and multiply, and we lose track of the truth.

The truth is that God knows what we're facing, and He has things under control. God is doing the very best for us from an eternal perspective. Even if we hurt now, in eternity we'll look back and say, "Wow, God really did the right thing for me." That's why verses like First Thessalonians 5:18 encourage us to "give thanks in all circumstances, for this is the will of God in Christ Jesus for you." And unless we believe this truth in difficult circumstances, we're going to run just like David did. Biblical truth grounds us in who God is so that we don't have to fear anything that comes against us. Don't forget what's true!

Don't Focus on Getting Relief

I think another reason David ran is that he started focusing on how to find relief from his situation. He started contemplating how he could work his way out of his situation. He started thinking and scheming, which led him to say, "There is nothing better for me than that I should escape to the land of the Philistines" (27:1).

How did David know that there wasn't anything better than that? Like any human, David was trapped within his own perspective. He didn't know whether or not he'd run into trouble living in the land of the Philistines. He didn't know whether or not God had a *better* plan for him than going to live among Israel's enemies. He just wanted immediate relief from his discontent; David was thinking of nothing beyond getting away from Saul. He was considering how good it would feel not to constantly worry about being killed.

We all, to a certain extent, do what David did. We evaluate our circumstances, and we come up with a plan that sounds good to us. There's glamour in the thought of an escape route. When we fantasize about how we could break away from our situations, eventually we will act on whatever feels best in the moment. It's like what happens when we put a candy bowl on someone's desk. It may take a few minutes or even hours, but eventually the person will take a couple pieces. In the same way, if we keep tempting ourselves with the possibility of an escape, then no matter how unhealthy our plan might be, we will eventually go for it. David put the "candy" of security out there, and he sat there and stared at it and thought about how nice it would be to relax. David wasn't supposed to run, yet he took off.

David should have known better. Remember his great-grandmother Ruth? She has an entire book of the Bible named after her. Ruth's mother-in-law was Naomi. When there was a famine in Israel, Naomi and her husband had failed to trust

God to provide for them in Bethlehem (which is ironic, because Bethlehem means "House of Bread"). They ran to Moab—the land of Israel's enemies. Sound familiar? Naomi's husband and two sons died, and eventually Naomi returned to Bethlehem. When the women greeted her, she told them, "Do not call me Naomi; call me Mara, for the Almighty has dealt very bitterly with me" (Ruth 1:20).

Even though Naomi had refused to wait on God and had run, she blamed Him for her misfortune. Those who had stayed in Bethlehem hadn't died of hunger; God had provided for them. It was because Naomi had listened to a lie that she had fled and ended up bitter. David knew this story, yet he failed to apply it to his situation. Like Naomi, he focused on finding an escape. Instead of waiting on God, he ran.

Don't Be Deceived by "Good" Results

Sometimes when we go our own direction, the results look pretty good at first. That's what happened to David. His plan appeared to work like a charm. He and his six hundred men went to Gath, and King Achish gave them the entire city of Ziklag to inhabit. Why in the world would the Philistines allow David to live in their land this time, when they had rejected him before? I think it's because the first time David came, he was a member of Saul's court; Achish knew that David was tight with the Israelites and probably thought he was acting as a spy. But by this time in the story, David had become a famous outlaw. Achish knew that David and Saul were at odds, and he knew that Saul was fearful enough of David to send an army of three thousand men after him.

David probably told Achish something like, "King Achish, I have been loyal to Saul my entire life and have saved his life multiple times. I've followed and obeyed him, yet he keeps trying to kill me. I'm done with him. If you receive me, I'll be just as loyal to you as I was to Saul." So David became Achish's right-hand man and lived in Ziklag with his two wives—Ahinoam of Jezreel and Nabal's widow, Abigail of Carmel. When Saul found out that David had fled to the Philistines' land, he gave up his search. That's just what David had been hoping for. He was safe from Saul, he had a house to live in, and he had a leader who trusted him. I bet David felt relieved and was patting himself on the back for a job well done.

Sometimes our self-made plans too yield immediate relief. When we decide to move ahead with our lives on our own, things can feel pretty good at first. We enjoy getting out of a trying relationship or a stressful job. It's like sowing a few seeds in the ground and immediately congratulating ourselves on the harvest. It isn't the planting but the reaping that counts. When we step out without God's blessing, we put ourselves in a dangerous place. It takes a while for those seeds to grow, and when they do shoot up, they don't produce beautiful blossoms. They're bitter, sour shoots. Just as going her own way left Naomi bitter, David's self-centered plan led him to a rough patch.

Don't Forget—Not Waiting Leads to Problems!

David found himself responsible for feeding the thousand or so people living in Ziklag. In order to provide enough food, David and his crew went out on raids against the Geshurites, the Girzites and the Amalekites. They killed everyone in the towns they came across so that no one could report back to Gath what had happened, and they carried off all the livestock and fabrics. David would then take the loot back to Achish and tell him he had raided Israelite lands—Judah or Jerahmeel or the Kenites. David still felt too strong a loyalty to his Israelite people to attack them, but he wanted Achish to trust him, so he lied about what he was doing and did his best to cover his tracks.

When we go our own way, we often end up in tight spots

that cause us to do things we would never do otherwise. David got himself into a sticky situation, and then it got worse. First Samuel reports, "In those days the Philistines gathered their forces for war, to fight against Israel. And Achish said to David, 'Understand that you and your men are to go out with me in the army'" (28:1). Achish made David his own personal bodyguard, and David vowed to go to fight against the Israelites, his own family and the people God had told him he would rule over some day. David was uncomfortable, but he had to put on a good front, so he told Achish he'd make him proud. Happily for David, the lords from the other Philistine cities were not comfortable having a Hebrew in their army. Achish told David that while he personally trusted David with his life, the other leaders didn't trust him, so he had to go back home (see 29:6–7, 9–10).

After faking his disappointment over not getting to fight, David and his men rode back to Ziklag. When they got close to the city, they saw that the entire town was on fire. While David and his men were gone, some Amalekites had come, taken all the women and children and ransacked the town. The men didn't know if their wives, sons and daughters had been killed. David's men—big, burly brutes—cried for their loss: "David and the people who were with him raised their voices and wept until they had no more strength to weep" (30:4). David hit bottom again. And what's worse is that his men spoke of stoning him because they were so upset over the loss of their children (see 30:6).

Think about it—David left Israel because he was afraid of one man, Saul, killing him. He went his own way and ended up in a town with six hundred men who wanted him dead. The bitter shoots were coming up. David's wives were gone, his men wanted to kill him, and his fellowship with the Lord was severely damaged and suffering.

Don't Wait . . . to Turn to God

Not waiting on the Lord is far worse than waiting. That's as true for us as it was for David. Over the years I've heard countless stories of people who didn't wait on God and who lost their families, jobs and money and ended up in a lot of pain. The only way these people came out of those dark periods was to do what David did when he hit rock bottom—turn to the Lord.

In First Samuel 30:6 we see that David completely reversed his direction: "David strengthened himself in the Lord his God." This is the first mention of God throughout all David's actions in the past three chapters. Faced with no real alternative, David took a step back and questioned God as to what He wanted for the situation. David started preaching to himself. He began to remind himself of real truth—that God is the majestic ruler of all mankind who loves us, cares for us and will do the very best for us. David went to God, admitted that his plan hadn't worked and asked for forgiveness. He had the priest, Abiathar, pull the ephod back out to ask the Lord what they should do.

David learned a huge lesson. He learned not to go unless God told him to go. He learned to focus on following God's plan of action rather than to take his own shortcuts. And he learned the importance of keeping God's truth at the forefront of his thinking.

God told David that he would succeed in overcoming the Amalekites, and that's exactly what happened. David and his men won a great victory—regaining their families and their flocks and laying claim to all the Amalekites' goods to boot. David sent the excess flocks to some of Israel's southern cities just to let them know that he was still around and that, according to what God had told him, he would one day be their king.

What a story of redemption! But it only ended this way because David repented of his foolish plan to go his own way and because God graciously accepted him back into His fold.

And if we're willing to return to the Lord, He'll save us from our own fallen ways as well.

Three Kinds of Waiting

I'd postulate that all people fit into three categories. First, there are those who have waited on God and who continue to wait, refusing to move unless God tells them to. They keep their eyes on the Lord's plan. The last part of Isaiah 30:18 applies to this group—"Blessed are all those who wait for him." God is being glorified in them.

Second, there are those who have tried to make their own way. They've lost sight of the truth that God's plans are the very best for them. They're filling their own needs for love by living together with someone outside of marriage. Or they're filling their needs for success by juggling the numbers at work or taking a shortcut to a promotion. Maybe they are filling their need for material things by going too deeply into debt for a dream house or a car. People in this group aren't following God, and they need to do what David did—take responsibility for what they've done, ask for forgiveness and begin waiting on God from this point forward. God never beats His children over the head with all the ways we've failed, but He does want us to ask His opinion on what He'd have us do. When we surrender our ways to Him, He leads us into His best for us.

The third group is made up of people who have been waiting, but not necessarily on God. They've been inactive, holding out for their circumstances to change. They feel captive and out of control. Circumstances can cause us to feel like that. People in this group have not taken things into their own hands yet, but they may be nervous and on edge, wondering and worrying about how their situations will end. It's as if they're driving on a freeway, boxed in by trucks. They can't see behind, ahead or to either side of their own vehicle. They're moving forward, but they don't feel safe—something isn't right. They may reach the right destination, but they're not going to get there the best way.

If we fall into this group, we need the peace and assurance that can only come from God. It's important that we draw ever closer to God. God is the ultimate ruler of the universe who has a perfect plan, and we need confidence from Him that He controls the convoy. Without that confidence we'll be tempted to break out of the box on our own. And that could lead to a serious accident. So draw near to Him. Remember, entrust your heart and your circumstances to Him, and rest in Him.

Whenever we feel overwhelmed by life's circumstances, we need to take a step back and remember that God is right there with us. His grace is enough to cover us. He wants us to trust Him and not have to go through what David did to learn the lesson. It's time for us to give up our escape plans, to stop looking for potential ways out of our circumstances. When we release control of our problems to God, He's strong on our behalf. The Lord honors those who rest in Him and wait on Him. We don't have to have it all together; we just have to wait, listen and trust.

Let's pray:

Father, we thank You for the gift of waiting, for we know that You work all things out for our good. Help us to be patient and to not become weary as we wait for Your promises to manifest in our lives. In Jesus' name, amen.

CHAPTER TWELVE

DAVID GIVES IN TO LUST:
OVERCOMING THE DESIRES OF A SEX-SATURATED CULTURE

2 Samuel 11–12

Pastor Marty Berglund

But the thing that David had done displeased the LORD.
2 Samuel 11:27

We live in a lustful culture. Just look at the magazines in the grocery store, watch a TV sitcom, go to a movie, or shop at the mall. Everywhere we look, our culture is promoting lust—pushing the idea that we should want more and more. We're daily confronted with images that tempt us to want pleasure in wrong ways.

Although our culture promotes lust, Christ-followers are called to avoid sexual immorality. God gives us commands in Scripture to be life preservers and rescue boats—to escape the damage lust causes (see 2 Peter 1:4). Whether we're actively struggling with lust or are only mildly aware of desires and temptations, we need to hear the Lord's warning: getting what we lust for won't actually get us what we want.

We're about to make a serious jump in our David timeline; many years have passed since the last chapter. Now Saul is dead, and David is about fifty years old and well established as Israel's king. He has many loyal followers, and he oversees a territory of sixty thousand square miles. Although there have been a few skirmishes, it's a relatively peaceful time. Israel is strong and financially secure. And in this context David does the stupidest thing ever.

Character Flaws

David was a good man, a righteous man and a national hero. He was known as a worshiper and a follower of God, yet at this stage of his life, he did something that deeply displeased the Lord. While David had made several silly decisions throughout his lifetime, this one in particular really messed him up. It all started with sexual lust. David acted on a desire that placed him outside the Lord's will and landed him in a painful, heartbreaking situation.

Second Samuel 11–12 tells a story of lust and betrayal—of David stepping out and taking what wasn't his. Even before this, though, David had been violating one of God's principles for years. Deuteronomy 17:17 says that no king of Israel should take multiple wives, "lest his heart turn away," but David had disregarded that warning. He had taken several wives, which might partially explain his lust for more women. When the Bible uses the term "lust," it's talking about sexual sin. Within marriage, sex is a righteous, holy expression of unity and love, but wanting sex outside the bond of marriage and following that want is lust. It's wanting more than God designed us to have, which puts our hearts in dangerous territory.

Wanting and Wanting More

Lust tells lies. Lust doesn't tell us that we'll pay for our actions later. Lust doesn't tell us that she'll get pregnant or that we'll end up with a dirty disease. Lust never tells us that we'll get a divorce. Lust doesn't remind us of our kids, our reputation, our plans. All it does is whisper that we should have *more, more, more*. It's almost like a drug addiction. We're never satisfied; we're always left craving the next fix.

David learned this firsthand. One hot evening David was feeling a little warm in his palace, so he stepped out onto his balcony, where a light breeze was blowing. He looked out over the houses and saw a beautiful woman—the Hebrew here says that she was "very beautiful"—bathing on her roof. David stood there staring at that naked woman, and he started wanting more. David already had several wives and concubines, but in that moment, as he saw what he was seeing, he wanted another woman, a different woman. King David bought into lust's lie. He told himself that because he was the king, he had the right to go after any woman he wanted. Rather than considering the consequences, he saw something he wanted and stopped at nothing to get it.

Years later David's son Solomon wrote, "He who commits adultery lacks sense; he who does it destroys himself" (Prov. 6:32). It's as if Solomon was giving his dad a lesson. And it's true. Getting what we lust for usually causes us to self-destruct. Just look at the lives of Hollywood's movie stars, of politicians and of the uber-wealthy; even though they've obtained money, fame and success, most of them are broken and unhappy and have traumatic personal lives. They got what they lusted after, but it didn't fulfill them. And what we lust for won't bring us the happiness and release we desire either. Instead, it will keep us from peace, a clear conscience and a pure relationship with the Lord.

More isn't better, and we never *deserve* the things we lust after. God has a better plan.

Run Away!

It wasn't David's fault that he wandered out onto his balcony and happened to see Bathsheba bathing. So what should he have done? When a guy sees something like that, it causes a switch to flip; it causes a sort of biochemical reaction. It can't be stopped; the only thing that can be done is what the New Testament says to do: Run! Flee! Get the heck out of there! Let's look at a couple passages.

First Corinthians 6:18 says, "Flee from sexual immorality. Every other sin a person commits is outside the body, but the sexually immoral person sins against his own body." Sexual sin is personal and defiles the body, which was created to be the temple of the Holy Spirit. We might not be able to change our feelings, but we can change our direction. Second Timothy 2:22 reads, "Flee youthful passions and pursue righteousness, faith, love, and peace, along with those who call on the Lord from a pure heart."

Listen—it's always possible to run. As a pastor, I've heard a million lame-brained excuses as to why people have messed up, when the truth is that these people didn't have to do what they did. They could have picked up on the warning signs and gone the other direction. The Bible tell us to flee, because the best way to "handle" temptation is to completely remove it.

David could have recognized that his switch was on and that he was sexually excited, and he could have gone to find one of his wives. I'm sure they weren't all busy. Or he could have redirected his energy into going fishing with someone or going for a walk or horseback riding. He could have turned and walked away. He had a million options, but he chose to fixate on an ungodly, unwise one, and it led to trouble.

The Consequences of Lust

A friend of mine who used to be the pastor of a large church out West discovered the repercussions of lust firsthand. He had been having some problems in his marriage, when he found himself attracted to one of the ladies in his congregation. Words turned to flirting, and flirting turned to the next thing . . . and soon he and this woman were having an affair. When what they'd been doing was exposed, he ended up losing his job. He tried to get another job and to pull his family back together, but everything fell apart. The next thing he knew, he was out on his own, living with another woman. He was walking away from the Lord's truths that he had preached for so many years.

After a few years, he got that new woman pregnant. She had a baby boy, and my friend lived with her for a couple more years until that relationship fell apart as well. He invested more into his new job and ended up making several million dollars. He met a wealthy woman in New York, and the two of them fell in love.

When this woman found out my friend used to be a preacher, she started asking questions about the Bible. As he explained things to her, he came under strong conviction. He cried as he presented the gospel to her. She prayed to receive Christ, and he decided it was time to get right with God. God helped him work through the shame and guilt of what he had done, but the pain remained. He said he thought he had been escaping the pain with his behavior, when all he had been doing was digging himself in deeper. He had put his children and multiple women through emotional trauma. He once admitted to me that he believed he would have been happier if he had stayed with his first wife and worked through their problems instead of lusting after escape, lusting after more.

That's what this story about David in Second Samuel teaches us. So rather than turning the other direction, David sent messengers to figure out who the beautiful woman was. He found out that her name was Bathsheba and that she was married to Uriah the Hittite. Because David had allowed himself to get worked up, he didn't give a second thought to her marital status. He called her to him, had sex with her and sent her home.

He thought he'd gotten away with the whole thing until Bathsheba wrote to him to tell him she was pregnant. But rather than admit his sin, David called Uriah home from battle so that he would sleep with Bathsheba and David could cover the whole thing up. But Uriah refused to sleep inside in his own bed while his men were still out in the fields fighting, which foiled David's plan. So David arranged for Uriah to be placed at the frontlines of the battle, and Uriah was killed. Once he was out of the picture, David sent for Bathsheba, married her and claimed her son as his own.

What David did was mostly behind closed doors. His lust, his sin, was hidden. He tried to cover his trail, but God knew what he had done. Second Samuel 11:27 says, "But the thing that David had done displeased the LORD." And then came the consequences.

The Lord sent the prophet Nathan to confront David. Nathan told David a story of a rich man and a poor man. The rich man had many flocks, whereas the poor man had only one little lamb that he treated as one of his children. When a traveler came to visit the rich man, the rich man slaughtered the poor man's lamb to prepare it for his guest. David was angered at the injustice of this story and declared that the rich man deserved to die for what he had done. Then Nathan hit him with the point: "You are the man!" (12:7).

Speaking through Nathan, the Lord told David that He knew exactly what had happened and that it had been dirty and wrong. A friend of mine who is a consultant for a big pharmaceutical company once told me that he had learned that if executives didn't learn to deal with their stuff privately, they'd end up having to deal with it publicly. That's exactly what happened to David. He tried to conceal his sin, but our God who brings all things into His light exposed them.

Because David had done what was evil in God's sight—taking more for himself after he had already been so richly blessed—

the Lord promised to bring calamity on his house. Nathan told David, "Now therefore the sword shall never depart from your house, because you have despised me and have taken the wife of Uriah the Hittite to be your wife" (12:10). The sword will never depart! That's a pretty awful prophecy for someone whom God had previously greatly blessed. Then in verse 11 the Lord declared, "I will take your wives before your eyes and give them to your neighbor, and he shall lie with your wives in the sight of this sun."

And both of these pronouncements happened exactly as Nathan had prophesied. David's son Amnon was lustful, just as his father had been. He raped his sister Tamar, and because of this action, his brother Absalom killed him (see 2 Sam. 13). Later, Absalom greatly disgraced David by taking all the king's concubines out on the palace roof and sleeping with them in the sight of all Israel (see 16:15–23). Finally, David and Absalom got into a big battle, and Absalom was killed (see 2 Sam. 18). *"The sword will never depart. . ."*

Second Samuel 12:15–18 says that after David and Bathsheba's son was born, the Lord struck him, and he fell ill and eventually died. David got what he lusted for, but the momentary pleasure he gained cost him years of strife. Acting on lust leads to serious consequences.

Hope for Every Sinner

Although David faced some dark days of separation from the Lord's blessings, there is some hope in this story. What Nathan said convicted David, and David cried out, "I have sinned against the LORD" (12:13). We might not get the full impact of David's repentance in that verse, but Psalm 51 offers a better picture of David's cry for cleansing and redemption:

> For I know my transgressions,
>   and my sin is ever before me.

Against you, you only, have I sinned
　　and done what is evil in your sight,
so, that you may be justified in your words
　　and blameless in your judgment. . . .

Purge me with hyssop, and I shall be clean;
　　wash me, and I shall be whiter than snow.
Let me hear joy and gladness;
　　let the bones that you have broken rejoice.
Hide your face from my sins,
　　and blot out all my iniquities.
Create in me a clean heart, O God,
　　and renew a right spirit within me. (51:3–4, 7–10)

David felt dirty and ashamed for months and years, and he wanted rid of his guilt. He couldn't get what he had done out of his mind, but he tried to cover it up so that no one else would know about it. Finally he admitted that God was the One against whom he had truly sinned. David knew he wasn't right with the Lord, so he asked God to clean him and to make him blameless. Although it took him a while, David finally did what he should have done from the start—he turned to the Lord and sought forgiveness, freedom from his sins and cleansing.

David's story reminds me of a time when a girl came forward to speak with a pastor after one of our church services, sobbing and shaking uncontrollably. She was in grief over what she had done the night before; she had slept with a man from the church out of wedlock. Odd as it may sound, I was glad she felt so awful about it, because it meant that she was right where she needed to be. I knew that the burden of her guilt and shame would lead her right into the Healer's arms. She wasn't trying to rationalize her actions; she was just breaking and coming before the Lord, asking Him to wash her clean. A couple years later she ended up marrying a wonderful guy, and now she has a great family. She's doing so well because she admitted that she was unclean and unrighteous, and God had compassion and cleansed and forgave her.

We're all guilty of committing atrocious sins that distance us from the Lord. But like this gal and like David, we can be saved and forgiven. But we need to come before the Lord with all our guilt and shame and to admit it if we've crossed lines we shouldn't have—mentally or physically. Lust will destroy us if we try to hide it, if we don't place it under God's convicting light and allow Him to heal our hearts and make us clean. We don't have to be controlled by our desires; God offers salvation.

Getting What We Need

If getting what we lust for doesn't give us what we want, then how *do* we get what we really need in life? Well, we see the answer in David's psalms. He wrote scores of psalms, praising and worshiping God for how good, great, loving and compassionate He is—and also complaining to God. David expressed his struggles, his enemies' unjust treatment of him and his hurts to the Lord.

How do we get what we really want? We start, as David did, by going to the Lord with everything. We follow the Lord's ways, and we live to do what the Lord tells us to do. Psalm 37:4 says, "Delight yourself in the Lord and he will give you the desires of your heart." When we give up our own way of pursuing delight, God fulfills us and gives us what we need most.

It's when people are waist-deep in sin and unable to even think about delighting in the Lord that they need to repent and get right with God. There is freedom in fleeing from wrongdoing. The Lord can wash clean every lustful condition. Like David, we have to confess to the Lord what we've done, and we have to admit that we need Him to heal us.

When everything in our life feels like it's falling apart and every direction seems wrong, it's time for us to own up to being lost. God can handle our admissions of anger and inadequacy. When we come before Him in honesty and humility, He is quick to forgive: "If we confess our sins, he is faithful and just to forgive us our sins and to cleanse us from all unrighteousness" (1 John 1:9). If we're willing to admit how we've fallen short and how we're tempted to fall short again, God will be quick to give us a clear conscience, a clean heart and a new perspective. Through His Spirit, He'll give us the strength to run away from the things that threaten to destroy us. He'll save us from falling prey to the lust that our culture promotes. When we delight in the Lord, He will give us our hearts' real desires.

Let's pray:

Lord, cleanse us completely of lust. Give us the strength to stand purely in the midst of a culture that promotes sexual sin and lustful desires, and help us to delight ourselves in You. In Jesus' name, amen.

CHAPTER THIRTEEN

DAVID GETS A HEART CHECKUP:
SEEKING GOD'S WILL THROUGH TRIALS

1 Chronicles 28–29

Pastor Glenn Kantner

The LORD has sought out a man after his own heart.
1 Samuel 13:14

Life is a series of trials and tests. We can't avoid them. Some people believe that Christianity is an easy pass to heaven and that being in the Lord ensures security and safety. In fact it's just the opposite. Christ promises us that we will face struggles and trials in this life (see John 16:33). What's hard for us to understand is that we *need* challenges to grow and sharpen our hearts. God uses tests in our lives to develop us and to prepare us for everything He knows we'll face.

David's journey to trusting the Lord was long and complicated, but through it he learned the importance of keeping a close check on his heart. When David sought to glorify God, his heart was naturally in the right place, but when he fixated on his own concerns, David got distracted and missed out on the Lord's best—and he ended up hurting others in the process. Thankfully, David sharpened his heart by regularly making the choice to trust God through *all* things. We too need to sharpen ourselves to be people after God's own heart.

After God's Heart: Keeping Our Hearts Healthy

David was anointed king early in his life, but it wasn't until fifteen years after his calling that he assumed the throne. Before that he had to fight several battles, and he ended up with a death warrant out on him that led him to flee from his homeland. Why? Because God knew that he wasn't ready to be king yet. David had to be built into what Israel needed and what God wanted from his life; he had to be sharpened.

What was God looking to build into David's life that would prepare him to be Israel's next king? First Chronicles, a book that covers David's final years, gives us a clue, and we'll see that it has to do with David's heart.

In chapters 28–29 David is seventy years old, and he is reflecting on his life. Thankful to the Lord for all that He had done, David decided to take a huge offering from the people in order to build a temple to God. But God told him no. He said that David was a man of war who had shed too much blood, so he couldn't build His temple—but He said that David's son could, and would (see 28:2–7).

David went ahead and gathered all the materials needed for the project and gave a big personal offering—110 tons of gold and 260 tons of silver. And all the Israelites brought their offerings—silver, gold, etc.—to the house of the Lord. David reflected on how God had enabled him to amass all that wealth and how God had united the country and increased the size and strength of Israel. Instead of being bitter that he couldn't personally construct the temple, David was honored that the Lord would leave that task to someone in his lineage.

David thanked God for blessing Israel so tremendously and for bringing the nation peace and power. He was full of gratitude for what the Lord had done. Look at David's prayer of thanksgiving:

Blessed are you, O LORD, the God of Israel our father, forever and ever. Yours, O LORD, is the greatness and the power and the glory and the victory and the majesty, for all that is in the heavens and the earth is yours. Yours is the kingdom, O LORD, and you are exalted as head above all.

Both riches and honor come from you, and you rule over all. In your hand are power and might, and in your hand it is to make great and to give strength to all. And now we thank you, our God, and praise your glorious name. (29:10–13)

David continued his prayer, paying close attention to matters of the heart:

I know, my God, that you test the *heart* and have pleasure in uprightness. In the uprightness of my *heart* I have freely offered all these things, and now I have seen your people, who are present here, offering freely and joyously to you. O LORD, the God of Abraham, Isaac, and Israel, our fathers, keep forever such purposes and thoughts in the *hearts* of your people, and direct their *hearts* toward you. (29:17–18)

And then David prayed for his son:

Grant to Solomon my son a whole *heart* that he may keep your commandments, your testimonies, and your statutes, performing all, and that he may build the palace for which I have made provision. (29:19)

In the preceding chapter, David had given Solomon direct instructions: "And you, Solomon my son, know the God of our father and serve him with a whole *heart* and with a willing mind, for the LORD searches all *hearts* and understands every plan and thought" (28:9).

What do we see in all this about what God was trying to build into David? David was focused on his and the people's hearts, because he knew that in order for them to be in God's will, his son and the rest of the Israelites had to ask the Lord to permeate their innermost being. That's true for us today as well. God is most interested not in military victories or community service but in the hearts of those who love Him.

All the circumstances and challenges that David faced strengthened his heart. David didn't have perfect faith; he failed and tried to fend for himself and made lots of mistakes. He didn't always do what God wanted Him to do. So why does Scripture call him "a man after God's heart" (see 1 Sam. 13:14)? Well, there were several things David did that were right.

After God's Heart: Doing God's Will

I know a pastor from the Philippines who says that being a person after God's heart means living life in harmony with the Lord. That means that what is important to Him is important to us, and what burdens Him burdens us. It means that when something goes wrong, we ask Him to help us change it, because we want to be in sync with His will. That's what this pastor calls "bottom-line Christianity"—the basic way to become like Christ.

When we choose to live that way, we're not in it alone. Second Chronicles 16:9 tells us that "For the eyes of the LORD run to and fro throughout the whole earth, to give strong support to those whose heart is blameless toward him." A man after God's heart has the Lord's strong support. That's what set David apart. Even though David occasionally lost his focus, in general he consistently sought the Lord's will. When he struggled, he always ended up turning to God. His psalms reflect his tendency to bring everything—the good and bad, his praise and pain— before his Lord. God wants to sustain us as He did David, but that can only happen if our hearts are open to doing His will.

Acts 13 reinforces the importance of having a heart that does God's will. In it the apostle Paul set up David as an example as he taught in the Jewish temple, giving the Jews the history of Israel—all the way from Abraham to Jesus, who came from the line of David to forgive everyone of their sins. In that process, Paul explained how God had removed Saul from the throne and installed David as king: "And when he had removed him, he raised up David to be their king, of whom he testified and said: 'I have found in David the son of Jesse a man after my heart.'" The very next phrase is He "will do all my will." Being a man or woman after God's heart means wanting to do what He wants us to do. David was set as an example of someone who submitted himself to be used by God. David was human and fallible; he just allowed God to use him. And God is still searching for hearts that will do His will 100 percent.

"Doing God's will" sounds wonderful, but we often equate that with following step by step instructions. God doesn't offer us a checklist on how to follow Him; He simply asks us to seek Him in all things. Being in God's will doesn't necessarily meaning working in the church or doing missions work in a foreign country. We don't see David directly ministering to others around him or preaching in the temple, because those things are not what God had called him to do. But remember what David said before he fought Goliath: "The battle is the LORD's" (1 Sam. 17:47). David fought for God's chosen people in God's name with faith that God would bring the victory. David listened to the Lord, fought the giant and won a physical victory with spiritual faith.

David gave 100 percent in everything he did and then entrusted the results to God. He didn't strive for fame or success; he just followed the steps the Lord laid before him and did his "secular jobs" with all his heart. He did everything with a heart to honor God: In his relationship with Jonathan, David fully committed himself, trusting his friend to help him see God's will. When he was camping in the cave and news came of the looting in Keilah, David asked God if he should go to help, and when God said yes, David went. David didn't kill Saul, because God's Word told him that it would be wrong. David learned to trust God in every facet of his life. He sought His will in his relationships, his day-to-day activities and his future plans. God looked at David's heart and saw a man who was willing to seek out God's will and to do whatever it took to follow it.

We should strive to have hearts that want to do God's will in every circumstance. For example, when we get in an argument with our spouse, are we saying, "Lord, what would You have me say in this situation? How can You love through me?" Or do we feel a need to air our grievances and "set the record straight"? When we're in a tough situation at work, do we want God to work His best for us and to redeem the circumstances, or do we want revenge? When our kids are already on our last nerve and then they deliberately make a huge mess, will we seek God's will then? When we land a big deal or get a raise and are feeling successful, will we ask God what He would have us do with the money? Or men, when our attractive female colleague approaches and is being overly friendly, will we follow God's will then?

I'm asking all these questions to get to the heart of the matter: are we truly willing to always respond to situations in a way that honors the Lord and follows His commands? The only way to have a heart right with God is to have a heart that is close to Him and seeks to do His will.

After God's Heart: Meditating on Who He Is

There's one problem with what I've been saying: it is not always easy to discern the perfect will of God. David had prophets who came and told him exactly what God wanted. But God doesn't always speak to people in that way. So how do we know what He wants us to do in specific situations? How do we reach an understanding of His will?

Recently I was reading the autobiography of George Müller, a man who I think had a good grasp on discerning God's will. Müller ran orphanages in London in the 1800s, and he was known as a great man of prayer. Whenever he needed funds or clothing or food for the children, he would simply pray, and God would miraculously provide whatever he needed. For example, he and the children would sit at the breakfast table and pray for breakfast, and somebody would knock on the door with food. He never solicited donations, yet he never went into debt; he provided for the children through faith and prayer.

What I found truly fascinating about Müller's autobiography is that he makes clear that all the miraculous ways God provided were nothing compared to knowing the Scriptures. He writes, "Formerly when I rose, I began to pray as soon as possible. But I often spent a quarter of an hour to an hour on my knees struggling to pray while my mind wandered." Müller knew something wasn't quite right. He realized, "The most important thing I had to do was to read the Word of God and to meditate on it. Thus my heart might be comforted, encouraged, warned, reproved, and instructed. . . . As my heart is nourished by the truth of the Word, I am brought into true fellowship with God."[1]

Müller gives us another example of a key man of faith who was focused on bringing his heart into close communication with God. Müller learned of God's likes and dislikes—His will—by meditating on Scripture. As he read the Bible, he would pause over each verse, thinking about every word. He said that his heart would always turn to prayer, but it was so much better when he started first by soaking in Scripture, because it helped clarify God's will in each situation. When we're immersed in God's Word, God's will suddenly becomes clear to us, even when we're dealing with a sticky situation.

We're not going to know God's will unless we're steeped in His culture. We learn God's ways by soaking in His truths, by getting His Word into us. When knowing Scripture becomes second nature to us, we'll know what God wants us to do when something comes up at the office or happens at home. When we have God's Word in our hearts, the Holy Spirit will illuminate Scripture for us, pointing out how we're following the Lord's commands or where we're straying off the correct path. First Corinthians 2:10 says that God reveals His wisdom to us through His Spirit. Through God's power we, like David, can be described as men and women after God's own heart.

The first thing God looks at when He examines our hearts is whether or not they're turned to doing all His will. He tests our hearts to prove them right and true. We too test things for the people we love. We want a certificate of authentication for the diamond ring we're buying for our future wife. We buy the vehicle history report on the used car we're getting for our son. God wants to prove our hearts in the same way; He wants to show that they're the real deal and are in good condition. He wants them to be tuned to Him so that His loved ones (us!) can experience close fellowship with Him. God doesn't test our hearts by holding a big club, waiting to see if we'll step out of line so He can beat us over the head and cheer, "Ha! I caught you!" No, He seeks to grow us. While He allows us to be tested, He also gives us all the tools we need to succeed, and He roots for our success. He wants us to have hearts that want to do *all* His will.

After God's Heart: Humbling Ourselves

A key piece to following God's will is placing everything He desires above everything we think would be best. We have to submit to God, admitting that He knows best. In Isaiah 66:2 the Lord says, "This is the one to whom I will look: he who is humble and contrite in spirit and trembles at my word." God approves of those who recognize who He is and who have an appropriate understanding of themselves as created beings.

When David was anointed king, he didn't go out and have a celebration declaring how great he was. Instead, he went back to tending his father's sheep. Nobody was around him out in the fields to pat him on the back and tell him how well he'd done, but that didn't bother David. Later, after David defeated Goliath and the people were declaring him their hero and singing songs about him, he didn't strut around town. He went back to doing what God had called him to do—playing the harp for King Saul. Through all his successes David stayed humble.

Of course, during some of the rougher times in David's life, he failed to keep God in His appropriate place. When David was afraid of what Saul might do, he fled; he didn't trust God to protect him. He certainly didn't do God's will when he lied to the priest at Nob or when he burned with lust for Bathsheba. But after each of those instances, David did something right; he confessed his sin and admitted that he had done wrong. He took responsibility for his sins. It takes a huge amount of humility to admit when we've royally messed up. It takes a huge amount of humility to take the blame instead of pushing it off on someone or something else. And David didn't just say that he was wrong—he repented, which is much different than simply admitting fault. Let me unpack how.

My extended family always gets together at Thanksgiving. One year my oldest grandson, Jackson, was picking on his younger brother. My wife finally looked at him and said, "Jack, you need to stop that and choose to be obedient." Jack looked at her and said, "It's too late, Grammy. I have sin in my heart. My heart wants to do the right thing, but my brain keeps making me do other things." He's a real five-year-old theologian. When we told Jack's mother what had happened, she said, "Jack is getting very good at confessing his sins, but we have quite a long way to go to repentance."

There's a huge difference between admitting that we're not perfect and repenting. Repentance carries the connotation of godly sorrow. It involves saying, "I have crossed a line that God had established, and now the perfect, pure, holy Ruler of the Universe knows that I have crossed that line and deserve to be punished." When we realize the severity of what we've done and completely turn away from our sin, God forgives us. That's what David did every time he messed up. And every single time, he was totally restored. I'm sure it wasn't easy to admit what he had done, but it was only because of his humble heart that David— despite all his sins—was able to be used by God.

Seeing the Value in Trials

It's not easy to believe that we need to be tested. It's tempting for us to pray for a happy-go-lucky, trial-free life. And yet is that really what we want, if it's going to make us weak and lead us away from Christ? We should be willing to face struggles if they will strengthen our faith and make us more like Jesus, the One whose love was so perfect and full that He faced death and separation from God in order to save us.

When parents take their baby to the doctor to get shots to strengthen its immune system and to protect it from something more serious, the baby doesn't understand. It just feels the prick of the needle, and it cries and wails to protest the shot until it's red in the face. And yet we know that in the long run, getting those shots is best for the baby. The child has to go through the pain to have a healthier future. We're like babies—screaming at God that His plan shouldn't hurt so much, crying that we'd rather not have the medicine. Yet God in His infinite love looks at us and says, "My child, I love you too much *not* to give you what you need—whether or not it's what you think you want. I love you too much to allow you to stay dull when you need to be sharp. I love you too much to leave you to a mediocre life when I've called you to perfect your faith."

The struggles we face are actually for our benefit. James 1:2–

4 encourages us, "Count it all joy, my brothers, when you meet trials of various kinds, for you know that the testing proving, or showing the genuine thing] of your faith produces steadfastness. And let steadfastness have its full effect, that you may be perfect and complete, lacking in nothing." God has a goal for us. He'd rather that we struggle and grow than stay comfortable and miss the joy of His fullness.

There's a great reward waiting for those who carry on with Christ. Second Timothy 2:12 says, "If we endure, we will also reign with him." Going through trials prepares us to be coheirs with Christ—to share in His kingdom reign! No one is already perfect enough to reign on his or her own merit. Even though Christ calls us to strive for perfection (see Matt. 5:48), He's aware that we'll never quite meet that standard in this life. The great part, however, is that when we ask the Holy Spirit to fill us, He works out that process in our lives, growing us into something more like God, into beings who reflects God's glory. We might call it sharpening with a purpose.

As Sharp As Christ

One summer we had a bad storm where I live in Medford, New Jersey. Rain flooded low-lying areas, and strong, driving winds knocked down a bunch of trees. I had several trees come down on my property, so I decided to go out with a chainsaw and chop them up. I revved the saw as high as I could and pushed down on the logs as hard as I could. Smoke blew out all over the place, but very few chips of wood flew off. Nothing much happened. I decided I needed to do something differently, because I felt as if it was me was getting chewed up instead of the wood. So I went out and bought a new chain for my saw. Once I had that baby installed, the saw sliced through the logs like butter; it hardly took any effort. I cut through seven logs in the time that it had taken me to work through that first one.

Chainsaw chains can be sharpened, but doing it is not an easy task; the chains don't seem to enjoy it very much. Putting it against a grinding wheel or file sends sparks flying, and the chain gets super-hot. I think we're kind of like those chains. We get worn down, dulled by the monotony of daily living. When we're not actively serving and growing, we get accustomed to inactivity, and we start rusting away. The beautiful, redemptive part of God's way of dealing with us is that God never just throws us away to replace us with a better Christian model. Instead, He chooses to sharpen us with the grindstones of loving our enemies and of facing trials. It's not pleasant—sparks fly and sometimes situations get pretty heated. But we come out of those tribulations refined and better able function as instruments in the Redeemer's hands.

Maybe, as we've considered the difficult seasons David faced, we've become aware of how God is sharpening us through our own situations. Maybe that challenging relationship at work is actually an opportunity to learn another facet of God's love. Maybe that person who pushes all our buttons is helping teach us a godly response to anger. Perhaps conflicts with our spouse due to our idiosyncrasies are God teaching us the value of the different perspectives of Christ's body. All our sharpening is an opportunity for us to be restored.

Searching and Restoring Our Hearts

When God restores us, it's like our sin never happened. That's why God could look at David and call him a man after His heart. Only because David sought forgiveness and forsook his sin could he be considered clean. God longs for us to humble ourselves as well, to bow before Him and admit that we've gone our own way and have hurt Him by rejecting His wisdom. He wants us to fall before Him—the King of kings—and seek His pardon. God wants this because He loves us. He knows that only when we seek His forgiveness can we enjoy freedom. We can be restored and washed clean.

God is searching our hearts. And when we see the true condition of our hearts, we long to get right with Him. Then God can bless us and be strong on our behalf. The Holy Spirit is here to lead us into all truth and righteousness (see John 16:13). I pray that the Lord will show each of us where we need to repent so that we can live more fully in Him. As we go through our weeks—paying bills, getting gas, running errands, driving to work—I pray that we will be conscious of the state of our hearts and will seek to be strengthened in the Lord.

This book ends here, but study of the Scriptures should not. There's still a lot to learn from the life of David, and the Bible is filled with other people's stories and important life lessons. Even though I read the Bible every day, I never stop learning new things, because God always has something new to teach and show me—and He wants to unlock His Word to all His children. We have the same opportunity that King David had to seek the Lord's will and to live in His fullness. When we seek the Lord's will through His Word, trust Him through all things and humble ourselves in repentance and prayer, we become people after God's own heart.

Let's pray:

Glory, Father! We thank You for the opportunity we have had to study the choices of Your servant, David. Thank You for opening our eyes to the conditions of our hearts so that we might be restored in You. In Jesus' name, amen.

Endnotes

Chapter 4

1. Lon Solomon, *Brokenness: How God Redeems Pain and Suffering* (San Francisco: Purple Pomegranate Productions, 2010), 79.

Chapter 5

1. A question always arises at First Samuel 18:10: How could an evil spirit have come from God? Is the text talking about an angel or a demon? Does the spirit come from inside of Saul? The answer is that we don't know for sure. Maybe this is similar to what happened to Job when God permitted Satan to work over him. But is there a real difference between *sending* an evil spirit and *allowing* one to attack? At any rate, God let it happen.

   Another possible answer deals with semantics. The word "spirit" can also refer to a person's disposition of mind or attitude. The word used in this verse for "spirit" can be translated that way. It could just mean that Saul had the wrong attitude. The word "harmful" can also be translated as unhappy, bad or sad. Perhaps Saul was depressed, or perhaps his anger and anxiety over the whole David situation welled up within him and changed his demeanor and spirit. There's no definitive way to tell, but the verse probably means one of these two things.

2. People often wonder what's going on with this whole foreskin deal (1 Sam. 18:25). Remember that First Samuel records a very harsh, very violent era of history that occurred over three thousand years ago. Now there was no media to

report the news back then, so it was common for soldiers to come back from war with proof of how many people they had killed. Saul's request that David prove he had killed a hundred Philistines was not that odd. What was odd was that he asked David to circumcise his victims. I submit that this was Saul's diabolical genius at work. Circumcision was a symbol for Israel's belonging to the Lord. I think Saul figured that he could either get David killed in battle, or if that failed, the surviving Philistines might get so angry over the insult of someone doing something to their dead men that their god hadn't commanded that they might put a hit out on David. I think Saul was just working to get David killed any way he could.

3.   I highly suggest that we read Richard Stearn's story in his own words in his book *The Hole in Our Gospel*. It's a phenomenal book that challenges us to evaluate whether we're truly striving to be a successful person in the Lord's perspective or whether we've become acclimated to America's concepts of success and comfort.

4.   "Whatever It Takes," Lanny and Marietta Wolfe, 1975.

Chapter 7

1.   In the Old Testament, when God gave Moses instructions to build the tabernacle, God instructed the priests to place twelve loaves of unleavened bread on a table and to replace the loaves with hot bread every Sabbath. One had to be ceremonially clean—not having had any recent relations with women—to eat the bread.

Chapter 9

1.   Craig A. Smith, *Sermon Illustrations for an Asian Audience* (Manila: OMF Publishing, 2004).

Chapter 13

1. George Müller, *The Autobiography of George Müller* (New Kensington, PA: Whitaker House, 1996), 139.

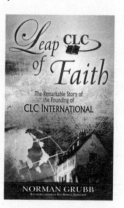

This book was produced by CLC Publications. We hope it has been life-changing and has given you a fresh experience of God through the work of the Holy Spirit. CLC Publications is an outreach of CLC Ministries International, a global literature mission with work in over fifty countries. If you would like to know more about us or are interested in opportunities to serve with a faith mission, we invite you to contact us at:

CLC Ministries International
PO Box 1449
Fort Washington, PA 19034

Phone: 215-542-1242
E-mail: orders@clcpublications.com
Website: www.clcpublications.com

DO YOU LOVE GOOD CHRISTIAN BOOKS?
Do you have a heart for worldwide missions?

You can receive a FREE subscription to
CLC's newsletter on global literature missions
Order by e-mail at:

clcworld@clcusa.org

or your request to:

**PO Box 1449
Fort Washington, PA 19034**

WATCHMAN NEE

OVER
1 MILLION
IN PRINT

THE
NORMAL
CHRISTIAN
LIFE

Starting from key passages in Romans, Nee reveals the secret of spiritual
vitality that should be the normal experience of every Christian.

Trade Paper
Size 5 ¼ x 8, Pages 255
ISBN 978-0-87508-990-4
$11.99

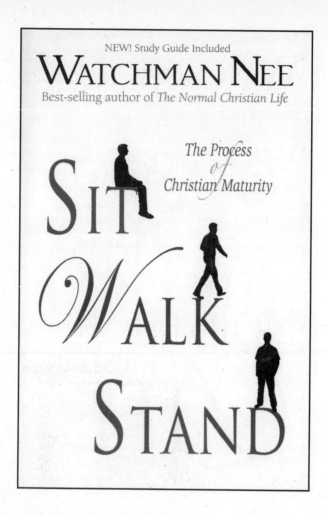

NEW! Study Guide Included

WATCHMAN NEE

Best-selling author of *The Normal Christian Life*

The Process
of
Christian Maturity

SIT
WALK
STAND

An inspiring look at Ephesians, opening our eyes to the process of Christian
living and maturity.

Trade Paper
Size 5 ¼ x 8, Pages 96
ISBN 978-0-87508-973-7
$8.99

"We all, with unveiled face, beholding the glory of the Lord, are being changed into his likeness from one degree of glory to another" (2 Cor 3:18, RSV).

WATCHMAN NEE

CHANGED INTO HIS LIKENESS

This book makes a valuable contribution to an understanding of God's way with His own people, through a study of the lives of Abraham, Isaac and Jacob.

Trade Paper
Size 5 ¼ x 8, Pages 90
ISBN 978-0-87508-859-4
$9.99

"STIRRING...ORIGINAL...PROVOCATIVE"

WATCHMAN NEE

LOVE NOT THE WORLD

A PROPHETIC CALL TO HOLY LIVING

Nee states that despite Satan's influence over worldly things, Christians must learn how to live in the world but not of it.

Trade Paper
Size 5 ¼ x 8, Pages 135
ISBN 978-0-87508-787-0
$8.99